Sociology of Diversity series

Series Editor: **David G. Embrick**,
University of Connecticut, US

The Sociology of Diversity series brings together the highest quality
sociological and interdisciplinary research specific to ethnic, racial, gender
and sexualities diversity.

Forthcoming in the series:

Disproportionate Minority Contact
How We Failed Children of Color
Paul Ketchum and **B. Mitchell Peck**

Race, Diversity and Humanitarian Aid
Black Ecologies and the Problem of Whiteness in New Orleans
Diana Harvey

Racial Diversity in Contemporary France
Rethinking the French Model
Marie Neiges Léonard

Out now in the series:

Beer and Racism
How Beer Became White, Why It Matters, and the Movements to Change It
Nathaniel Chapman and **David Brunsma**

The Death of Affirmative Action?
Racialized Framing and the Fight Against Racial Preference in College Admissions
J. Scott Carter and **Cameron Lippard**

Find out more at

bristoluniversitypress.co.uk/sociology-of-diversity

Sociology of Diversity series

Series Editor: **David G. Embrick**,
University of Connecticut, US

Find out more at
bristoluniversitypress.co.uk/sociology-of-diversity

SOUTHERN CRAFT FOOD DIVERSITY

Challenging the Myth of a US Food Revival

Kaitland M. Byrd

BRISTOL
UNIVERSITY
PRESS

First published in Great Britain in 2021 by

Bristol University Press
University of Bristol
1-9 Old Park Hill
Bristol
BS2 8BB
UK
t: +44 (0)117 954 5940
e: bup-info@bristol.ac.uk

Details of international sales and distribution partners are available at
bristoluniversitypress.co.uk

British Library Cataloguing in Publication Data
A catalogue record for this book is available from the British Library

ISBN 978-1-5292-1141-2 hardcover
ISBN 978-1-5292-1142-9 paperback
ISBN 978-1-5292-1144-3 ePub
ISBN 978-1-5292-1143-6 ePdf

Cover design: blu inc
Front cover image: unsplash.com – Elevate

For

Mom and Dad

Contents

Acknowledgments

First, I would like to thank David Embrick for encouraging this project and helping me think through what Southern craft food diversity means in the modern South. I would also like to thank my wonderful editor Shannon Kneis for helping guide this project from inception through finished product, as well as the anonymous reviewer whose feedback made this a stronger book. Finally, I thank the Southern Foodways Alliance for their effort in putting together the amazing oral history archive that made this project possible.

I was lucky to be a visiting scholar at the National Center for Institutional Diversity (NCID) at the University of Michigan while writing this book. The support of NCID was invaluable. Thank you to Tabbye Chavous for extending an invitation to be part of NCID and facilitating many wonderful conversations across campus. Dana Brown, thank you for your encouragement and support in every phase of this project. I also want to thank Ching-Yune Slyvester, Marie Ting, and Charlotte Ezzo for their support as I transitioned into the center.

I also need to thank my parents for their ongoing support of my work, even when it takes me far from home and Brenda Patton who is always encouraging of each new project I take on. I want to thank Megan Alibaruho, Carrie Dedrick, Tina Brockman, Danielle Wyand, Megan Segoshi, Oliver Rollins, Susan Cheng, and James Hammond for the many virtual happy hours that took place during the spring and summer while I was writing and that helped me find the balance during those difficult days of the stay-at-home order.

Although writing a book feels like a solo endeavor, cloistered in a separate room alone with my laptop, most of the writing for this book took place after Michigan locked down in response to the pandemic. I spent the following months in a small apartment with my laptop and my partner who was writing his own book during the stay at home order. Carson, there is no one else I would have wanted to be quarantined with as our book deadlines approached, and the world paused. I love you and thank you for your patience as this book took up most of my time and energy. I look forward to many more culinary and wine tasting adventures in our future.

Series Editor Preface

In 2021 we face new challenges such as navigating life during the COVID-19 pandemic and trying to figure out if our lives will ever resume the way things were prior to the pandemic. And the fight for racial and social justice continues as we hear new stories of police brutality against black and brown folx; more anti-immigration rhetoric from mostly right-wing politicians but generally across the board; and whitelash against perceptions of a changing tide that would presumably alter the status quo capitalist, patriarchal, white supremacy society in which we reside. In the midst of all of this, new ways of invoking the amorphous and ambiguous terms of diversity and inclusion have been produced at all levels of society. For example, we continue to hear more discussions in higher education and other institutions about the need and importance of diversity without ever discussing what that diversity is. Further, on the other end of the spectrum, we have seen political attacks on diversity such as a 2020 presidential executive order banning diversity training from transpiring in anything Federal government related. Of course, the latter is dangerous. However, I have argued elsewhere that superficial rhetoric on diversity is equally dangerous as it fuels hope without substance. This book series interrogates how widespread and perverse diversity ideology has become in our society. The first two books in this series—*The Death of Affirmative Action? Racialized Framing and the Fight Against Racial Preference in College Admissions* (2020) by J. Scott Carter and Cameron D. Lippard, and *Beer and Racism: How Beer Became White, Why It Matters, and the Movement to Change It* (2020) by Nathaniel G. Chapman and David L. Brunsma—open up readers' eyes to the sociological realities of policies, institutions, and culture. In the first book the authors contend that the persistent fight against affirmative action in the US has become a rallying cry for conservatives to maintain the status quo; the idea behind the fight is that we have become a post-racial society and affirmative action policies and practices are essentially anti-white. In Chapman and Brunsma's book, the authors argue that in order to truly understand the beer industry, and particularly the fast-growing craft beer industry, one must understand its roots in whiteness and white supremacy—that whiteness and racism have operated and continues to operate in all aspects of the beer industry.

In this third book published in the *Sociology of Diversity* series titled, *Southern Craft Food Diversity: Challenging the Myth of a US Food Revival*, Dr Kaitland M. Byrd continues the line of peeking behind closed doors, borrowing the language of prominent late sociologist Peter Berger, to tease out southern food craft, culture, and notions of authenticity. Specifically, Byrd argues that the idea of mostly middle class, college educated white men (and sometimes women) who have been immortalized and paid homage as great cultivators and revivalists of food art and culture dismisses the more complicated histories and realities of the rise and fall of craft food trends and the producers, some of whose families descend from a long line of artisans whose livelihoods depended on not just their products and crafts, but the culture of farm to table that has been heavily co-opted. In doing so, Byrd covers a broad swath that includes southern winemaking, coastal fishing, local markets, cured meats, and the whitewashing of southern food restaurants. The reader is thus exposed to a more complete history and detailed analysis of the hidden inequalities of food, the importance of place and space, and how stereotypes fuel existing racial and gendered perceptions of groups in society, particularly of the South, while allowing other groups (read: white men) to reap rewards as they reinvent existing food crafts and culture. This is a must read book, particularly for anyone interested in better understanding how, through stitching together sociologies of culture and inequalities, we can better tease out how food and the cultural meanings behind food are sometimes more complicated than how they are typically presented.

David G. Embrick
University of Connecticut

Introduction: Crafting Revisions from Southern Food Culture

In 2018, The Inn at Little Washington became the first and only restaurant in the Washington, DC, region to receive three Michelin stars, arguably the world's highest rating in the fine dining restaurant industry. Michelin stars are awarded by the Paris-based guidebook based on anonymous reviews surrounding the atmosphere, cuisine, and entire dining experience of a restaurant. The 2018 guidebook listed 104 restaurants in the world holding the coveted three Michelin stars. Of those restaurants, only 14 were located in the United States, with a majority located in major metro areas such as New York City, Los Angeles, San Francisco, and Chicago. The Inn at Little Washington appears to fit the positioning as a fine dining restaurant located in one of the United States' most important and influential cities.

Yet The Inn (as locals and industry insiders often refer to it) is not located in Washington, DC, or even in one of the affluent suburbs of Virginia or Maryland. The *Michelin Guide* for the region provides many helpful maps for patrons to use to find highly rated restaurants. For each restaurant, the map that has the location of the restaurant is noted with the entry to make it easier to find your way to a table. However, for The Inn, the map notation is "N/A" because you literally must travel off the guide's maps, down Interstate 66, then traverse country highways for another 40 miles to reach it (Michelin, 2020). As the sprawl of suburbs fades into farms and wineries, travelers will enter Rappahannock County, one of the least populated counties in Virginia, and find The Inn at the center of the county seat, Washington, noted as "the first of them all" after being planned by a young George Washington in 1749. Similar to when The Inn opened in 1978, cosmopolitan travelers could easily describe it as existing in the middle of nowhere. Despite its fairly remote locale, however, people from around the world come to dine at The Inn, including visiting dignitaries, entertainers, and culinary celebrities. Culinary royalty Julia Child dined at The Inn, and when Queen Elizabeth II visited Virginia for the 400-year anniversary of Jamestown and the founding of the Virginia Colony in 2007, Patrick O'Connell, the chef, founder, and owner of The Inn, prepared a meal with wine pairings, the entire meal sourced from Virginia farms, purveyors, and wineries (BBV, 2007).

Granted, Virginia is located in the Southern United States, but why am I starting a book about Southern food with a brief look at an award-winning fine dining restaurant known for elegance, opulence, and elite clientele? Simply because The Inn at Little Washington was one of the first restaurants of an emerging fine dining culinary scene in the US that cultivated what foodies flock to today: farm-to-table dining experiences complete with craft food and beverage. For over 40 years, chef Patrick O'Connell and The Inn have sought to "convey a sense of place at The Inn by making use of the abundance of wonderful products from the region, which the French call a 'cuisine de terroir'" (The Inn at Little Washington, 2020). Before there was an entire movement around farm-to-table cuisine, before craft and artisanal became descriptors for food, and at a time when the most popular seasonal, farm-to-table restaurant in the United States was Alice Waters' Chez Panisse in Berkeley, a restaurant emerged in a renovated gas station in a town with fewer than 250 residents in the middle of nowhere in Virginia helmed by a self-taught chef. The Inn would become the first and only restaurant in the South to win the highest culinary award in the fine dining world by using products mostly sourced from local farmers and purveyors.

The Inn at Little Washington eschews the stereotypes long held in people's imaginations and experiences with Southern food. Barbecue, fried chicken, and vegetables cooked within an inch of their life in bacon grease is a common perception about the everyday food of the region; morels with freshly made gnocchi and lamb carpaccio are not envisioned as "Southern" food. Yet morels, lamb, freshly made pastas and preserves, and yes, barbecue are all part of the local food and agriculture scene. Southern food today, as it has for generations, includes artisanal products, heritage meats, and heirloom grains resurrected from the past, bringing the taste memories of previous generations to modern consumers (Jordan, 2015).

Southern food is often characterized by unhealthy, fried foods and a limited number of vegetables, and the South is home to many of the most popular fast food chains in the country including Chick-fil-A, founded in Georgia, Kentucky Fried Chicken, founded in Kentucky, and the quintessential Waffle House, also founded in Georgia, as well as several other fried chicken chains. The South is also home to soda giants Coke, founded in Georgia, and Pepsi, founded in North Carolina. While the South has produced more than its share of unhealthy food, captivating the palates of people across the world, it has also produced trailblazing chefs who focused on seasonal, farm-to-table ingredients before farm-to-table was popular.

Chef Edna Lewis, the grandchild of freed slaves, spent her childhood surrounded by the rhythms of nature and observed how it impacted the food on her family's table in a rural Virginia community filled with the descendants of freed slaves. As an adult she left Virginia, first for Washington, DC, then New York City, finding work as a laundress then a seamstress and eventually a restaurant chef. Her cookbook *The Taste of Country Cooking*, published in 1976 by Judith Jones, the same editor who published Julia Child's *Mastering the Art of French Cooking*, was the first of its kind to present Southern food as a celebration of seasonality, grounded in Lewis's experiences living in Virginia and foraging for wild greens in the spring or the communal hog killing in the fall. Although seemingly common today, with Southern chefs publishing cookbooks organized by season or highlighting vegetables, in 1976 the South was still marred by the poverty and racial inequality that were showcased in the news, including Lyndon Johnson's War on Poverty and the CBS documentary *Hunger in America*, airing in 1968, that showed the South suffering from the effects of poverty and poor nutrition. It was within this context that Lewis published her cookbook and started to change the narrative of Southern food to include seasonality, but more importantly to bring women of color back to their rightful place at the table as autonomous chefs. Her work resonated with industry leaders including Alice Waters and James Beard, as well as fellow Southerner and famed *New York Times* food editor and critic Craig Claiborne (Franklin, 2018).

Edna Lewis took popular and often negative conceptualizations of Southern food as fried and unhealthy and turned them on their head to reflect the Southern food of her youth, seasonal and fresh, that continues to resonant with Southern chefs today, including 2019 James Beard Award winner Mashama Bailey, whose time in France coupled with her readings of Lewis's cookbooks led her to argue: "The only place in the States that seemed to have anything in common with the French lifestyle was the South. ... In France we prepared a gratin of summer vegetables; at Grandmamma's house, she made squash casserole" (Bailey, 2018, p 196).

Edna Lewis's influence means that today a consumer does not have to look to the new hip restaurants in Atlanta or Charleston to find chefs showcasing local Southern products such as Virginia wines or Carolina shrimp. Instead, restaurants across the South, including Mashama Bailey's Savannah restaurant, are highlighting local products sourced from producers who are not the educated white middle-class, almost exclusively male, purveyors found in New York City and other large urban areas across the nation who seek out the craft movement as an alternative to a desk job (Ocejo, 2017). In many cases these producers are third- and fourth-generation crafts people who are continuing family traditions that have recently seen more success as the craft and local food movements draw consumer attention to the products that have always existed but were not necessarily seen or desired.

This book explores the ongoing changes to foodways and food culture, especially across the Southern United States, by grounding the South in discussions within the sociology of culture and food studies more generally to explain the abundant attention given to craft or artisanal industries that were originally established to make it possible for struggling rural communities to establish a degree of financial stability. Although this craft movement is relatively new in the major urban areas of the US, the South is unique in hosting restaurants and food producers who never stopped using these techniques but have long been ignored. By tapping into consumers' desires for local and slow food, these traditional preparation techniques and products are placed into the sphere of food as a form of an art world and thus embedded with knowledge that could be lost if people stopped practicing these techniques. The majority of these producers are not the white, upwardly mobile producers found in urban areas and given a large amount of media attention and Yelp reviews, but instead they are working-class men and women from a variety of racial and ethnic backgrounds who rely on selling their products to sustain their families.

Modern Southern foodways

Southern food is among the most distinct and uniquely American food cultures. However, the diversity embedded in Southern food is often ignored in favor of a white male-dominated version of Southern foodways. This reality calls to mind the same racial politics of white-tablecloth, haute cuisine restaurants across the country. As sociologist Gary Fine (1996) explains in his work on restaurants, professional kitchens have a long history of gender and racial inequality, with women being in the front of house, commonly as waitresses and hostesses, while white men are typically chefs and line cooks, and the lowest levels of the kitchen hierarchy such as dishwashers are filled by people of color. This inequality reflects household inequalities, with home kitchens remaining the domain of women, who are mothers and wives and are overwhelmingly responsible for the care work within their families, and women of color, who were historically responsible for the domestic tasks of middle- and upper-class whites, while still taking on these tasks for their own families when they return home from work (Sharpless, 2010).

As American studies professor Marcie Cohen Ferris (2014) explains in her account of food's power in creating the modern South, although the South offers insight into how traditional foodways survived and are now experiencing a culinary renaissance, a discussion of the South must first include the acknowledgment of the region's complex and problematic history of inequality. Race relations throughout the South from slavery through Jim Crow relied on the forced labor of blacks to put food on the tables of wealthy whites. As enslaved communities infused their food memories into meals and Indigenous communities had not just their land, but their crops and foodways, stolen and coopted with the expansion of the US, a new food culture developed in the South (Twitty, 2017). These developments, coupled with the poverty and hunger historically dominating the rural South and the mountains of Appalachia, forced many Southerners to either rely on their own skills and knowledge for gardening and preserving food to make it through the winter or purchase cheap, often inferior food from local stores.

This historical trajectory resulted in Southern foodways representing one of the only examples within the US of a distinct food culture, produced by the daily interactions between white and black Southerners as well as Indigenous communities, along with the more recent settling of Asian and Pacific Islander populations and Latinx immigrants. Although the South is often viewed through the lens of the past, characterized by distinct racial lines only encompassing whites and blacks, stark rural poverty, and strict conservative religious and political leaders, the modern or New South presents a very different perspective on the lived reality since the end of the Civil Rights era (Edge, 2017). As Jennifer Jones (2019) elucidates in her work on relationships between black and Latinx residents in Winston Salem, North Carolina, the New South is continually shaped by new immigrants from Mexico and by the return of black and white families whose ancestors had left the South for the industrial meccas of Detroit and other Northern cities. These historical and current shifts in population demographics create a more diverse and far more complicated picture of the southern US than stereotypical images of the region rooted in the Antebellum era allow. As these groups moved either away from or back to the South, they brought their foodways with them, making it possible for Southern food to spread as blacks migrated out of the region (Latshaw, 2013).

Despite the presence of these diverse groups and their shared affinity for music and food, the South's failure to deal with poverty, racism, and other related problems has created a region that is both old and new, continually plagued by old problems of poverty and racism and infused with new waves of immigration, anti-immigration politics, and poverty that no longer leads to hunger and emaciation but instead to obesity and diabetes (Edge, 2017). Yet it is only through the process of understanding the New South and the problems often grounded in historical wrongs that the region can move forward to embrace its current vitality and increasing diversity, with modern Southern foodways serving as a hallmark of this New South.

In the past 20 years, the South has experienced a culinary renaissance with elite chefs opening restaurants in Charleston, South Carolina, Nashville, Tennessee, and New Orleans, Louisiana, among other urban destinations. While these restaurants have spurred the revitalization of farming in the South and the rediscovery of heirloom crops such as Carolina Gold rice, long thought to have disappeared, and brought the region into the national spotlight for the quality and uniqueness of its food, this popularity often fails to look beyond the restaurants of award-winning chefs. Outside the increasingly hard-to-get-into restaurants run by elite chefs, another version of Southern food exists. In small towns across the region, food producers, winemakers, and shrimpers continue to bring life to traditional techniques by balancing the knowledge required to safely produce a product, such as wine or homemade jam, with the art of making something other people will want to buy because of its quality and taste, and with the skill required to make a living from the sea or land. These producers are rarely the upwardly mobile chefs we have come to recognize from their frequent appearances on the Food Network or other televised cooking specials (Collins, 2009). Instead, these are hardworking people who battle Mother Nature on a daily basis to carry on their family traditions, such as shrimping or farming, as their main source of financial security. Yet it is the products created, raised, or caught by these men and women that are the ingredients featured by elite urban chefs within and far beyond the South.

It is in this context that craft food exists. Although craft food commonly refers to a value-added product produced by hand outside the industrial context, such as craft beer or a craft cocktail, that definition extends to trades grounded in the past such as barbering. All these jobs require a specific set of skills, once mainstream but undesirable because of the labor required, that have since become desirable jobs (Ocejo, 2017). As sociologist Richard Ocejo (2017) argues in his work on craft industries, the use of craft-based techniques reflects not only the finished consumable product, such as a craft cocktail, but the cultural knowledge required to elevate a seemingly common product, such as a haircut, into a cultural experience that is only accessible to the culturally aware consumer who desires a unique and authentic product. In this context, extending the definition of craft beyond value-added products, such as wine or country ham, to encompass the producers and purveyors of raw products, such as shrimp or vegetables, makes it possible to examine both stages of craft production, because in both cases consumers have the ability to interact directly with the shrimper at the dock or the winemaker in a tasting room.

The broader definition of craft to include both raw and value-added products existing outside the industrial or mainstream production system also aligns with Heather Paxson's (2013) work with cheesemakers who raise the animals whose milk makes the cheese; she argues separating the cheese from the animal creates a disconnect reflective of mainstream production, where each piece is assembled separately and all the pieces come together to be assembled in a distinct location. Paxson found that the cheesemakers argue the final taste of the cheese is dependent on the experiences of the animal who produced the milk, and to separate out that knowledge is to produce an inferior product that contradicts the consumer's desire for an authentic product and the producer's desire for a holistic product.

The popularity of the local and slow food movements in the US has raised consumers' awareness of where their food comes from as well as the process involved in making it. The current movement began as part of the larger countercultural movements of the 1960s and 1970s, when participants sought out healthy and environmentally friendly alternatives to mass-produced food options (Blay-Palmer, 2008). Over five decades the slow food movement became foundational to numerous business ventures and increased takeover of small businesses into large scale conglomerates (Miller, 2017). An example of this occurred in 2017, when corporate giant Amazon purchased Whole Foods for $13.7 billion (Green, 2019). During the early 2000s consumer demand for local and organic foods rose further, as evidenced by the increasing number of farmers' markets in the US, surging from 2,000 markets in 1994 to over 8,600 markets by 2019 (Helmer, 2019).

The increasing demand by consumers to know where their food comes from, coupled with the increasing national recognition of

Southern food as a unique cultural field, simultaneously extends *and* weakens the diversity and inclusion embedded in Southern foodways. Food movements and the solidification of regional foodways intersect around health, culture, and economic demands to determine how inclusive a food culture appears as opposed to how diverse it is on a day-to-day basis. The South has a long history of racial diversity and oppression, but the interactions between groups means Southern foodways are the product of centuries of interactions to a point where it is hard to discern where one influence stops and another starts. However, as the South becomes increasingly urbanized, this knowledge is at risk of being lost or being housed only in elite restaurants with high-dollar price tags instead of at the small roadside stands throughout the region where it exists today, as it has for generations.

Barbecue has many of the hallmarks of a craft Southern food: many pitmasters maintain relationships with local farmers who provide their restaurants with fresh vegetables or hogs, and the recipes are often family recipes that avoid the use of processed ingredients (Byrd, 2019). The skill required to be a pitmaster aligns with the skills required to be a shrimper or a winemaker, involving a complex balance of knowledge regarding nature and science to produce a final product that can then be purchased by a consumer. Rodney Scott, a barbecue pitmaster, won a James Beard Award for Best Chef: Southeast in 2018, making barbecue "one of the South's simplest foods" to receive this national recognition (Purvis, 2018). Although barbecue fits into the concept of craft food, this book goes beyond discussing traditional Southern foods such as barbecue with its long-established racialized and gendered dynamics.

Instead, I examine a variety of food products including wine, cured meats, seafood, and preserves as well as restaurants and businesses reflecting a wide array of ethnic traditions and origins to show the diversity embedded in Southern foodways that shatter the stereotypical assumptions that "everything is fried down here." In many cases, these craft foods are not only traditional to specific places, but they also represent a source of economic stability in a region that continues to struggle with poverty. The intricate dance between traditional claims of authenticity and underlying inequalities highlights how diverse modern Southern foodways are and can continue to be if we look beyond the popular conceptualizations of Southern food as battered, fried, and covered in butter, or led by mostly white men as elite chefs, to acknowledge and hold up the marginalized communities often ignored as keepers of heritage foodways far from urban locales.

Craft and authenticity

How can Virginia support over 300 wineries and vineyards? Why are shrimpers in New Orleans still talking about the Deepwater Horizon (also known as BP) oil spill? Why does the presence of homemade jams and pickles spark debate at farmers' markets? How can one type of country ham be better than another, especially when it is triple the price? How can tamales be a staple on menus throughout the Mississippi Delta? These are a few of the multitude of questions asked about Southern food culture. Food is a unique cultural product. Its life span is often only as long as a meal lasts and reflects broader cultural contours around what we eat and the meanings we give to the ingredients that find their way to our bowls, plates, and the end of our forks. As a cultural product, food is embedded within a complex structure, nestled within and reflective of the broader cultural contours and inequalities of a given society (Belasco, 2002).

This book draws on the intersection of authenticity and inequality in sustaining food traditions while acknowledging producers' resiliency to adapt to changes in production facets including technology, regulations, industry and organizational structures, occupational careers, and market conditions (Peterson and Annad, 2004). Regardless of the seemingly new uniqueness embedded in the craft movement, the knowledge and skills required to produce artisanal foods are not new and have remained integral to Southern foodways despite economic constraints. In fact, the diversity of foodways, and life in general, throughout the South illustrates the influence of inequality through institutions, market pressures, and stereotypes, among other societal forces, that reify narrow views and approaches to the region's communities and people (Huber, 2008; Stanonis, 2008). Unlike many urban areas, where craft foods can easily be found in farm-to-table restaurants and craft cocktail bars run by elite chefs or bartenders, craft foods across the South are central to the farmers' markets, the docks and highway stands in coastal communities, and the small roadside restaurants dotting the landscape. The producers of craft foods are not only the white, upwardly mobile, educated chefs found in major tourist destinations; they are farmers, winemakers, shrimpers, and restaurant owners of a variety of races and ethnicities who rely on the production of craft food products for their livelihoods.

Craft or artisanal food products are experiencing a rebirth across the United States. As consumers become increasingly concerned about the health and environmental impacts of what is on their plates, they begin to push for more slow and local foods to exist in opposition to the industrial agricultural system and heavily processed foods (Blay-Palmer, 2008). Although this is predicated on bettering the food system, it remains embedded within social inequalities, as those who are privileged to seek and often produce these alternative products are often middle- or upper-class, young, educated whites living in urban areas throughout the US (Cairns and Johnston, 2015; Finn, 2017; Bowen, Brenton, and Elliot, 2019). The success of this movement has led to the revitalization of "craft" foods. From craft cocktails to artisanal jams and cheese, the desire for nonindustrial foods has made it economically feasible, and profitable, to create restaurants and businesses aimed at avoiding anything industrially produced in favor of local handmade or craft products (Miller, 2017).

Over the last 20 years, a resurgence of craft food industries has occurred in the United States. Drawing on consumers' desire for slow and local food, craft breweries, traditional butchers, cheesemakers, and bakeries have been popping up across the country (Paxson, 2013). These industries are typically found in major urban areas, staffed by middle-class, college educated, often white men, and sometimes women, who view working in these industries as part of an alternative lifestyle existing in opposition to the mainstream emphasis on industrial consumption (Ocejo, 2017). However, this emphasis on urban craft industries obscures the complex reality behind the craft food movement outside major urban areas and the diverse communities that have supported craft and artisanal foods as both art and necessity. Across the South these slow and local foods are a traditional part of daily life, and their continued practice sits at the intersection of financial sustenance, knowledge, and art. By exploring a variety of Southern artisanal foods, from Virginia wineries to shrimping in coastal communities and kimchi in Houston, and the producers of these foods, this book shows how traditional, not necessarily "new," these movements are within the region. Arguably, it is the diversity of those who are central to these products and foodways that renders it and the related history invisible to most US consumers.

Unlike other forms of art, once food is consumed or has spoiled it is gone forever. Although cookbooks and recipes leave lasting documentation regarding specific ingredients and processes and thus offer a guide to complete a final dish, that does not mean two people using the same cookbook will end up with identical results. Variations in ingredients, personal taste, and available cooking equipment can all impact the final outcome of a dish, even when two cooks start from the same point (Jordan, 2015). Instead of trying to produce identical dishes, chefs and other food producers rely on sensory memories or embodied nostalgia of culinary memories to recreate dishes from the past. As Latinx literature and food studies professor Meredith Abarca (2017) argues, these sensory memories are the knowledge taken from the private sphere, mostly mothers' knowledge in the kitchen, and recreated in a new geographical location and time, typically the public sphere of a restaurant. Although these culinary memories are frequently discussed in regard to populations who engage in some type of border crossing, often in terms of Mexican immigrants within the US, it offers a framework for understanding the importance of memory as it relates to taste across people and places (Garcia, DuPuis, and Mitchell, 2017).

These culinary memories play out in restaurant spaces where chefs work to create dishes grounded in their personal taste or edible memories of a time and place often distant from the present reality. When done successfully, culinary memories serve as a connection not only for the person creating the final dish, but also for consumers who are seeking out those experiences and flavors from their own culinary memories but are unable to replicate them (Vazquez-Medina, 2017). This culinary nostalgia, while commonly discussed in reference to immigrant populations who are able to maintain connections to their country of origin through the senses associated with the cooking process, also occurs among craft producers who are relying on their taste memories and processes taught to them by previous generations (Jordan, 2015). One of the goals of this book is to explore how this culinary nostalgia overlaps with impression management to produce craft foods in Southern ethnic restaurants as well as in craft food production more broadly.

An important consideration is how people consider one form of food to be a representation of a cuisine, a community, or a culture. Considering sociologist Richard Peterson's (1997) discussion of the fabrication of authenticity in art worlds and culture as a form of impression management (à la Erving Goffman [1959]), cultural products are continuously evolving through a reciprocal process between producers and consumers in which groups of actors are continually altering their definition of authenticity as production conditions and consumer demands change (Hughes, 2000). This perspective allows us to further consider how craft producers understand their products as existing at the intersection between historical taste memory and modern claims of authenticity grounded in perceived sincerity and originality, both of which reflect changing production conditions and consumer demands (Peterson, 2005). Simultaneously, this framework acknowledges that what is considered authentic is continually changing, and as Goffman argues, the self is the continual negotiation between the front and backstage of everyday life, and authenticity is the relational product of this impression management on the part of the producer to ensure the product's financial success (Hughes, 2000).

Southern Craft Food Diversity uses authenticity grounded in the process of impression management as a framework to go beyond the urban centers and open up the traditions, or taste memories, and knowledge embedded in craft foodways of the South by discussing the men and women responsible for their continuation and historical preservation not found under the city lights. These communities are not the elite, upwardly mobile white chefs or "hipsters" with their well-manicured beards and tattoo collections often associated with the craft or local food movements. Instead, many communities central to historically embedded craft and local food movements spanning hundreds of years in the South are poor and working-class shrimpers, farmers, and restaurant owners whose families have melded Southern foodways with their own ethnic and regional understandings of food culture and its meaning in everyday life. By problematizing authenticity as a process and not an innate aspect of a product, I am able to amplify the experiences and life histories of craft food producers to act as a lens into the ongoing impression management embedding a product within authenticity as the social context, specifically the consumer demand, surrounding the product change.

A brief note on methods

This book uses the transcripts of oral histories from 176 people who keep Southern foodways alive but are often ignored by the popular food movements in the US and the media attention given to them. The collection of oral histories from people across the South occurred between 2006 and 2018 as part of the Southern Foodways Alliance's (SFA) oral histories project (Southern Foodways Alliance, 2019). The SFA is housed at the University of Mississippi and works with the goal of documenting, recording, and preserving the diversity found within Southern foodways, while honoring the chefs and producers responsible for the labor behind Southern food.

Five industries (winemaking, fishing, farming, curing, and professional kitchens) across ten states (Arkansas, Georgia, Kentucky, Louisiana, Mississippi, North Carolina, South Carolina, Tennessee, Texas, and Virginia) are featured in the succeeding chapters. This scope of what constitutes the South matches John Shelton Reed's (1986) conceptualization of the South as any state that is a former member of the Confederate States of America, which can easily be extended to include Delaware, Maryland, Oklahoma, Texas, and Washington, DC. The South, and those who call it home, reflect a particularism that is different from the rest of the United States and shapes the identity and culture of the region, and it continues to exist both within the geographic boundaries of the region and with those who once lived in that shared space (Ferris, 2013; Latshaw, 2013).

Seventeen oral histories were collected from winemakers across Virginia, Georgia, and North Carolina. A total of 55 oral histories were collected from shrimpers, boat makers, chefs, and others connected to the fishing industry from Mississippi and Louisiana on the Gulf Coast, and Virginia and the Carolinas on the Atlantic Coast. The farmers represented in this book include 38 farmers from Georgia, Mississippi, and North Carolina. The curemasters are from Kentucky, North Carolina, Tennessee, and Virginia, totaling 19 people. The final chapter includes the oral histories of 47 people from a variety of ethnic backgrounds and countries of origin, many of whom have been in the United States for less than 25 years and live in Arkansas, Kentucky, Mississippi, North Carolina, Texas, or Virginia (see Appendix for more demographic information on the oral history participants).

The oral histories were coded in a three-step process. The first round of coding was a line-by-line reading of each oral history with a focus on recurring themes with a sensitivity to claims of authenticity and inequalities. The recurring themes were then treated as sensitizing concepts to create a more formal coding scheme that was then refined with a subsequent reading of the oral histories. The frames centered on what was discussed and in what context they were mentioned, while the themes run through a majority of the oral history (Altheide, 1996). The third step was the comparison of frames and themes within and across industries.

Each industry was coded separately and is discussed in its respective chapter. Although there were many thematic overlaps across all five industries, employing the same coding scheme would have caused the nuance within each industry to be lost. The similarities within the themes are discussed holistically in the concluding chapter, in favor of a more encompassing narrative of the nature of work in the South within each individual industry. This makes it possible to highlight the regional importance of each craft food industry to the larger understanding of diversity embedded in Southern foodways, through first a nuanced understanding of the industry followed by a more holistic discussion of Southern foodways.

Book layout

Southern Craft Food Diversity sheds light on the rise and fall of craft food trends through an exploration of artisanal Southern foods and their producers who exist outside urban centers and popular tourist destinations. Many of these producers descend from a long line of craft and farm-to-table families who made these products not just for business, but to survive. Further, many of these families share a lineage marked by marginalization and oppression, which is reinforced by their outlier status in the burgeoning craft industry today. Popular trends directly impact the food appearing on plates throughout the nation and the world, but there is little attention on how those trends develop or the underlying inequality shaping who is at the heart of producing these foods and sustaining the foodways. This book presents an example of the rise of food trends through the concerted effort by their producers to maintain traditional preparation techniques despite continual economic, environmental, and health pressures.

Chapter 1 explores the modern-day appearance of wine in the South. One of Thomas Jefferson's agricultural dreams was to produce wine from Virginia soil similar in quality to what he had found in France. Although he failed for the most part, and subsequent pests and Prohibition decimated the grape vines that were left in the area in subsequent eras, there are over 300 wineries operating across the state today. This chapter explores the rebirth of the wine industry in Virginia and North Carolina, the states with the largest wine industry in the South. This exploration of the re-emerging wine industry of the region shows how winemakers are tapping into increasing demands for local and regional products while also exploring the demanding economic and working conditions required to run a successful winery. Yet almost all these wineries rely on tourism and the local community and exist in opposition to the industrially produced wines found for sale at most stores. These wineries also serve as a gathering space for their patrons to develop a sense of community while consuming the product.

Chapter 2 looks at the role of shrimpers in the availability of local seafood. From hurricanes to oil spills, the coastal South must cope with many difficulties of depending on the sea for one's livelihood. Within these communities scattered across the bayous and barrier islands are engrained food traditions and knowledge emphasizing the importance of the sea and its provision for families and Southern foodways. However, these communities' existence is tenuous due to past tragedies that continue to impact the lives of the fishermen and restaurant owners long after the devastation has faded from national headlines. The success of these communities is often dependent on chefs and consumers in major urban areas demanding local or regional products instead of cheaper, industrially produced alternatives.

Chapter 3 situates the experiences of women who sell their goods at farmers' markets within the social and historical context of the region. Southern food culture, like the restaurant industry in general, is rife with gender inequality. Women, whether white or black, were traditionally relegated to labor within the home. This work included cooking at a time when processed food did not exist and before the introduction of modern technology such as stoves and refrigeration units. Everything was made from scratch and ensured a family was sustained throughout the year. Despite the trend toward processed foods in the 1950s, rural areas across the South maintained a degree of traditional cooking techniques and canning practices. In most cases this was out of economic necessity, but it shaped the development of Southern food culture, leaving lasting marks. Today, farmers' markets offer a space for the sale of these traditional value-added products. This chapter addresses how the resurgence of a culture and subsequent spaces catering to slow and local foods makes it possible to revalue traditional food preparation techniques, specifically farming, canning, and baking from scratch, by placing them into the space of alternative productive relationships and embedding them with value as a form of knowledge and art, instead of isolating them within the exploitive and oppressive space of capitalism.

Chapter 4 examines the process of curing meats, which was originally done out of necessity to preserve meat before the advent of refrigeration. Today, those same methods are practiced across Kentucky, North Carolina, Tennessee, and Virginia, where preserving meats, especially country ham, is an art form. However, despite the current financial success and popularity of select companies known for their hams, these families turned to curing meats because it was a way to make money in difficult financial times. In a region known for its farming communities, country hams and other specialty cuts of meat have survived changing agricultural and health codes without losing touch with the flavors and traditions that make these products unique.

Chapter 5 looks into the communities across the South that are responsible for infusing Southern foodways with their individual ethnic foodways. From the Lumbee Tribe in North Carolina to the Chinese grocers in Mississippi and the Latinx population in Kentucky, these groups have all left their marks on the food traditions of the South yet are often absent from discussions of traditional Southern food. An aspect of marginalization is the invisibility of life and history, because it distorts the perception of who is important for cultural traditions and how they relate to structural inequalities. This chapter focuses on how these communities have navigated the balance between producing traditional foods and replicating taste memories for themselves and their consumers, all while coping with the inequality and discrimination that continues to impact these communities today. This chapter showcases how racial and ethnic minorities are integral to Southern foodways and its history, not outliers to it.

The Conclusion places Southern foodways and the inequality embedded in traditional representations of it into conversation regarding the increasing media and tourist attention garnered by popular Southern foods. While financially advantageous to some producers, these trends reinforce the financial hardships along with many racial, ethnic, class, and gendered stereotypes faced by communities who are integral to these foodways and traditions. This final chapter explores the diversity embedded in Southern foodways—if we choose to look beyond the popular stereotypes—and discusses the future of the restaurant industry in light of the coronavirus pandemic.

Terroir in a Glass: The Rise of Southern Winemaking

I grew up in what is today labeled the Northern Virginia American Viticultural Area (AVA), a designation given to established wine regions based on the shared environment that contributes to the final taste of the wine or terroir. Yet these established AVAs and the plethora of Virginia wineries (over 300 at the beginning of 2020) are a relatively new phenomenon on the East Coast. Before most of the vineyards down the road from my childhood home were planted, the region was known as the edge of Washington, DC, and horse country, where cows outnumber people, and wine was not yet on the cultural radar. One Friday evening in the summer as a young teenager, I was left at home while my parents went to a dinner party I wasn't allowed to attend. Less than 30 minutes after my parents departed for the party, my father returned and quickly rummaged through the pantry for several bottles of wine before leaving again. The party had begun with a wine tasting of a bottle each of red and white wine from the two wineries in the county where I lived. After trying each wine and subsequently pouring it out on the grass, my father decided to go home and get a couple of bottles he knew were good from long-established California wineries. Suffice it to say, the local wines that evening were not "up to snuff," as my parents would say, and could have easily been confused with "purple vinegar" or syrup.

Several years later I returned home from college for the summer and found a job at one of the local vineyards less than a mile from my home. The work was less than glamorous; most people who romanticize the life of winemakers as tasting wines overlooking a vineyard watching the sunset often miss that wine is an agricultural product, and thus you have to get your hands dirty. We worked outside in the vineyard maintaining the vines to ensure the budding grapes were able to receive the proper amount of sun, shade, and specific spray to ensure growth and prevent pests. We tended the vines Monday through Friday for the entire months of June, July, and most of August. Virginia summers are filled with high heat and high humidity, with temperatures often well above 80 degrees Fahrenheit, or 27 degrees Celsius and a heat index that steadily increased as the day progressed. The only reprieve from working outside in the scorching sun came on bottling days, when instead of going outside we stayed in the tank room, where wines were stored in large metal tanks before either going into oak barrels, as with the chardonnay and cabernet franc, to age, or directly into bottles, as with the sevyal blanc. The room was always cool, almost cold, to ensure the tanks were kept at the proper temperatures. On these rare days, fewer than a dozen each summer, we watched as empty bottles were quickly filled and placed into boxes to receive labels, with the pungent smell of wine filling the room as it gently splattered on hands or clothing as we cleaned the bottles. Working behind the scenes at a winery was far removed from the elegance of the tasting room, where customers came in through the large oak doors and stood at the dark oak wine bars to swirl and sniff the variety of wines being offered that day.

I turned 21 my first summer working at the winery, and a few weeks later my parents and their close friends, who had hosted the dinner party years before, all came to the winery for my first official wine tasting. They all loved a variety of the wines we tasted that day, compared with those they had tasted that summer evening many years before. Now, when I return home, we'll often go wine tasting and enjoy the carefully crafted, and now celebrated, wines of the region. Today, 11 wineries, one meadery, two breweries, and two distilleries exist in my home county, with at least two vineyards under construction and many more people exploring the possibility of starting their own. These many opportunities to explore craft and artisanal beverages exist in a county without a single stoplight and with fewer than 7,500 people. Despite its remote locale, it offers a chance to disconnect and partake in the growing wine culture of Virginia.

Every weekend driving down the main highway through the county you will glimpse the importance of the wine industry to the region. Each dirt or gravel road leading up to a winery has a steady stream of cars entering and exiting, many with out-of-state tags, but mostly people hailing from Washington, DC. Yet these spaces are a blend of agricultural life and escape from reality. Most of the vineyards are tucked into the rolling hills of the region with rows of grape vines dotting the landscape, and the narrow dirt and gravel roads leading up to tasting rooms often overlook the scenic views of the Blue Ridge Mountains and Shenandoah Valley. While a few of the wineries have magnificent tasting rooms that could host hundreds of people simultaneously, most are smaller ventures that boast picture windows, small fireplaces, and large patios where you can often see the winery owners' home in the distance as well as the livestock that occupy the acreage not planted in grapes.

Although the wine industry in Virginia is relatively young, the state's wines are slowly gaining national and international recognition. One of Thomas Jefferson's agricultural goals was to produce wine from Virginia soil similar in quality to the wine he had tasted abroad, particularly in France. Although for the most part he failed, and subsequent pests and Prohibition decimated the grape vines that were left in the area, today there are more than 300 wineries and vineyards operating across the state. The subtle history of winemaking in the region suggests, contrary to stereotypes of the people and food culture of the Southern US, that there's more in the rolling countryside and in the glasses of locals than sweet tea. This chapter explores the rebirth of the wine industry in Virginia, North Carolina, and Georgia, the states with the largest wine industries in the Southeast. Through this exploration of the region's re-emerging wine industry, I show how winemakers are tapping into increasing demands for local and regional products while describing the importance of the demanding economic and working conditions required to run a successful winery. Almost all these wineries rely on a delicate balance of tourism and the local community. These wineries exist in opposition to the industrially produced wines found for sale at most stores resulting from the corporate takeover of California's famed Napa Valley (Conaway, 2018). These wineries also serve as a gathering space for their patrons and members of the winemaking community to enjoy the literal fruits of their labor and develop a sense of community.

Southeastern wine

Although the East Coast has a stable wine industry, ranging from the Finger Lakes region of New York to the established AVAs of Virginia and the muscadine grapes of the Carolinas and Georgia, they are decades behind the established wine industry of California. However, their history goes back to the earliest days of the nation, to the time when the states were still British colonies. The wine industry in the Southeast is varied, with particular emphasis on the type of grapes grown in each state. Grapes, like other agricultural products, are very susceptible to variations in the sandy soil, climate, and terrain, all the things making up the terroir or taste of a place that is often mentioned in discussions of wine (Veseth, 2011). These differences can lead to certain varietals growing better in some areas compared with others. For example, the muscadine grape grows well in the soil and extreme heat and humidity of Georgia, while the more delicate chardonnay grows well in the soil of Virginia, which has good drainage. Despite the differences across Southeastern wineries, they are a growing industry and tourist destination. In Virginia alone, the wine industry contributed $750 million to the state economy in 2013 (Carter, 2013).

Virginia wine

You cannot discuss Virginia winemaking without talking about Thomas Jefferson. A majority of the wineries will tout this historic connection to their product, which often includes a discussion of the history of wine in Virginia and Thomas Jefferson's desire to produce wine at Monticello. Although Jefferson is credited with introducing the desire to produce wine in Virginia, the Jamestown colonists were required by the King of England to plant grape vines for wine (Carter, 2013). Wineries across Virginia frequently refer to Jefferson's dream and subsequent struggles. Felicia of Oakencroft Winery explains: "Thomas Jefferson was a visionary in his time. He had a vineyard ... and he, unfortunately, because [of] the things that we've been suffering with the late spring frosts, he was never able to make wine at Monticello. But certainly, his influence was felt." Her winery sits as part of the Monticello appellation, which encompasses Charlottesville and the surrounding area, along with 25 other wineries in 2008. Although Felicia has since retired and the winery has closed, the Monticello AVA she helped establish is still a dominant force in the Virginia wine scene. As of 2019, there were 46 wineries included in the Monticello AVA designation. Jefferson's dream of producing wine at Monticello failed also in part because of a disease called phylloxera that killed grape vines. It was not until grafting vines (that is, taking new rootstock of grapes such as merlot and viognier and grafting them onto rootstock resistant to the disease) became common practice that classic varietals, such as chardonnay and cabernet franc, could be grown on a large scale in Virginia soil (Zecevic, 2018).

Although he failed to consistently produce wine, Thomas Jefferson's desire to start a winery in Virginia continues to influence Virginia wineries and the wine culture of the region. As you drive up the winding dirt road through acres of vines covering the rolling hills of Barboursville Winery, you can look off to the right as you near the wine tasting room and see the stone ruins of an old plantation house connecting the winery to Thomas Jefferson. Melissa explains the connection between the estate's original owner, James Barbour, and the Founding Father: "We also have Governor Barbour, who was a contemporary of Thomas Jefferson's—the ruins of the house are here on the property, and Thomas Jefferson designed it. It was one of only three residences that Thomas Jefferson designed." Barboursville also sells Octagon, their unique blend of Bordeaux varietals and their most expensive wine. The bottle's label gestures toward the winery's connection to Virginia's history, with a replica of the estate plans for James Barbour's house, designed by Thomas Jefferson in 1814. The label features the drawing of the first floor of Barbour's house, and in the center is an octagonal-shaped drawing room, from which the iconic wine draws its name.

Although *vinifera* grapes, the main source of Old World wines and table grape varieties, struggled in Virginia until the 1970s, like the rest of the Southeast the state has a successfully grown native grape: the norton. Dennis explains the origins of the norton grape: "Norton was basically, or is, a native grape of Virginia. It was selected by Dr. Norton in, I think, about 1835, somewhere in that area, and was actually the backbone of the Virginia wine industry up until Prohibition." Although the norton is a native grape, only a handful of wineries in the state currently produce a norton wine, including Dennis's Horton Winery. The use of the grape has seen a resurgence in recent years, however, led by wineries' continued desire to deepen their connections with Virginia winemaking history and the terroir of the state.

The early struggles of the Virginia wine industry were not limited to pests and disease. The Department of Agriculture and Virginia Tech, today known for its viticulture program that helps winemakers get started and deal with any new environmental problems, were also opposed to the establishment of wineries in Virginia. Gabriele, an Italian-born winemaker brought over by the Zonin family who founded Barboursville, explains how much of a struggle it was to start a Virginia winery in the 1970s:

> I went to visit the Commissioner of Agriculture in June of '76. ... He pulled out a box with a cigar and he said, "The future of Virginia is tobacco and not wine." ... There were two dozen scientist from Virginia Tech and from the USDA each explaining what I was doing didn't make any sense and couldn't be successful. ... I told the commissioner, "I'm sorry that you had to disturb so many people to tell

me to go home, but I'm in the Land of Freedom, and I don't disturb anybody, so I should be allowed, I think, to continue with my experiment." And the professor from Virginia Tech said, "As long as you throw away your money or the money of the people you work for, that is perfectly all right with us. The moment you get a Virginia farmer excited about something that doesn't make any sense, we have a moral duty to stop you."

In the late 1970s, Barboursville received the fifth winery license in the state. Tobacco settlements, decreasing sales, and increasing supplies from overseas meant farmers needed to find an alternative crop. By 2004 tobacco subsidies had all but disappeared and farmers began switching to wine. Other wineries, including Jim Law's Linden Vineyards, sit on former apple orchards, while farmers and growers have turned to vineyards to replace the raising of livestock (Myers, 2000).

Unlike in other Southern states, Virginia's wineries are not in agreement on their identity as Southern wineries. Felicia, one of the first women winemakers in the state, explains how she sees Virginia's wine industry:

> Well, I don't think here in Virginia we think of us as Southern wineries. I mean, I think that's more south of our borders. We think of ourselves as part of the whole explosion of wine growing that's taken hold all across the country, and we have had tremendous influence with Barboursville and the Italians coming here, and we have French investors.

The plethora of wineries and wine influence in the state, as well as the lack of a prevalent native grape, led some winemakers to see Virginia as a unique winemaking area, while others, including Dennis, focus on Virginia's historical role to cement the wine's Southern identity: "I think it's absolutely a Southern wine, and believe it or not we are really south of the Mason–Dixon. I think some of the wine style is made for Southern food as well because we are in Virginia." Virginia's historical geographic location is enough to make its wines Southern.

Although Virginia wineries are relatively new, with most appearing since the early 1990s, many still try to retain the connection with the local community:

> We try to deal with as many local people as possible. If Luca needs to have part of the field bush-hogged, he's always

> going to hire somebody that's a local guy. ... I think it's long before the Green Initiative and just doing this that's been the way of life in Virginia for hundreds of years and it's just kind of started being noticed.

Melissa, of Barboursville, explains that the idea of sourcing products and services locally is not new, especially in a region where agricultural communities had to rely on what they could produce and on their neighbors for survival. Even within the wine industry, the youth of Virginia wines facilitates a camaraderie among winemakers that no longer exists in more established wine regions, such as Italy. As Virginia wines have improved, the overall image of Virginia as a legitimate wine destination has also improved, as it is currently the sixth largest producer of wine in the United States (Carter, 2013).

North Carolina and Georgia wine

Although Virginia is known for Thomas Jefferson's dream of producing wine, North Carolina has its own history that some argue goes back to when the states were just starting to be settled as colonies by England. Dave, of Duplin Winery, explains the origins of the muscadine grape in the state:

> The Mother Vine is the world's oldest living grapevine, and it is reputed to be over 480 years old. It is located on Roanoke Island, the Lost Colony. ... They say that Sir Walter Raleigh's colonists actually ate grapes off of this vine, and in the 1800s a winery called the Mother Vine Winery opened and incorporated that vine and others that were growing in the area.

Duplin exclusively produces muscadine wines, with over 40 varieties available at their three tasting room locations. While a majority of those original vines have been lost, the Mother Vine still lives on Roanoke Island. Although the history of North Carolina wines is as historically entrenched as Virginia's, the major difference is the type of grapes used in winemaking. Jefferson and Virginia focused on *vitis vinifera*, varietals native to the Mediterranean such as vidal blanc and merlot, while North Carolina capitalized on native grapes *vitis rotundifolia*, also known as the muscadine grape, which grows throughout the Southeast. The muscadine grapes' thicker than normal skin makes it less susceptible to fungal diseases caused by Southern summers (Brown, 2017).

Terroir, or the connection between taste and place, can be seen in the success of the muscadine grape in North Carolina and Georgia. Unlike the more recent arrival of *vineferia* grapes in Virginia, muscadine grapes have long been present in the Southeast because they can grow wild, and winemakers remember being able to go into the woods as children and pick muscadine grapes. Robert explains:

> The muscadine has always been with us but you had to find a market for it. I always tell people, the muscadine—you have to go back to the catfish in Mississippi. We grew up on the farm where you went down to the creek; this time of year, you can get all kinds of catfish because they was in the mud hole. But they all would taste mud, but once you started taking the catfish out of that environment and putting them in a clean environment you had seafood; now everybody wants catfish. The same way with muscadine: once you cultivate them and manage them, they become more tasty and more available and that's what makes them more popular. Also, the muscadine can only be grown in the Southeast of the United States, this is a native grape to this area. That's a big plus right there.

He grew up with wild muscadine grapes growing in the woods around his family's property. Although the grapes grow wild, their market success depends on careful cultivation and winemaking processes that are integral to Robert's success at Tilford Winery in Georgia.

The need for such cultivation of muscadine grapes and for winemaking techniques made it somewhat challenging for North Carolina to gain respect for the product during the early days of production. Dave, a strong supporter of muscadine wine, explains the early distaste for growing the native grape:

> We did find early on there was a lot of bad-mouthing going on; a lot of folks stuck their little pinky up and said, "We are going to open a winery that makes *vinifera* wines because we want to show people that North Carolina makes something better than that sickly scuppernog junk."... But now we are finding those folks are also getting into the muscadine business.

Although the initial dislike of muscadine grapes meant that only a few wineries were growing them, over time the increased awareness of the grape and subsequent consumer attention has led other wineries to grow muscadine grapes, although most only offer one or two types of muscadine wine in comparison with Dave's 40 varieties.

Despite the dislike some winemakers have for muscadine grapes, others recognize the unique history and properties of wine based on native grapes. Bob, of Hinnant Winery, explains why he chose to focus on the uniqueness of the muscadine: "I've heard, before Prohibition, North Carolina was the largest wine-producing state in the country, and it was muscadine and it was not anything else. It's a good grape; it's a Southern grape. ... It's just unique; it's fruity, sweet, very aromatic and that's the best way I can describe it." The history of the grape coupled with its unique taste facilitates the connection to other iconic Southern products, as Dave explains:

> [Muscadine] only grow[s] in the Southeastern United States. ... It's something special that only grows here. We want them to talk about Duplin wine like they talk about Maryland crab cakes or Duke's mayonnaise. If you're a Southerner you can drink RC Colas and you're going to use Duke's mayonnaise and you're going to drink Duplin wine, we hope, and watch NASCAR.

The popularity of the muscadine grape, aside from it being a native grape, also connects to the identity of the South. Charlie explains why he, and his family's Georgia winery Still Pond, decided to focus on the muscadine grape:

> Our wine is for the simple Southern, for a Southerner who likes muscadine grapes, likes the way it tastes, who isn't going to turn his nose up to something just because it is from the South. ... Like my father says: we were raised on Coca-Cola and sweet tea so we like a sweeter wine.

Several soda companies have their origins in the South: Coke was founded in Atlanta, Georgia, while Cheerwine and Pepsi are both based in North Carolina. Charlie connects the preference for sweeter drinks, like soda and sweet tea, to set the stage for a preference for a sweeter wine, such as muscadine.

While muscadine wine is identified as a sweeter, regionally specific grape in comparison with the *vinifera* grapes, it has also been the basis of scientific debate regarding health properties that extend beyond the recommendation to drink a glass of red wine a day (Brown, 2017).

Sonya, of Garden Gate Winery in North Carolina, explains: "The muscadine grape has—it's very beneficial for lowering cholesterol and for high blood pressure. They're doing a lot of research in it. They're coming out with the seed pills and, hopefully, it will be a breakthrough in medicine." The result of these findings has been an increased market for muscadine wine. Dave explains how the market has changed since the original research was publicized:

> Campbell University came down and tested these muscadine wines because all the tests are on *vinifera* grapes, and we're looking for this resveratrol [a powerful antioxidant found in muscadine grapes]. ... They came back with very positive results and showed that muscadine wines had seven times more resveratrol in it than the other grapes. ... Since that article in 1996, we've been able to sell every bottle of wine we've made.

Dave's Duplin Winery also sells freeze-dried seeds of the grapes, which have been put into soaps and shampoos because of their antioxidant power, along with grape seed capsules that are supposed to act as anti-inflammatory agents. The health properties of wine add to its marketability, with the North Carolina Muscadine Growers Association (NCMGA) outlining five key health benefits including reducing signs of aging, strengthening immunity, regulating high blood pressure, reducing cardiovascular disease while also improving heart health, and reducing cancer risk (NCMGA, 2020).

Georgia, like North Carolina, is also known for the muscadine grape. Robert, of Tilford Winery in Georgia, explains the difference between the muscadine and European grapes: "Muscadine is a native grape of the US, so you can't crossbreed it with the European grape, which is the *vinifera* grape, so the basic thing that we use [is] the Southern type grape, which we call the muscadine, which is in the *rotundafolia* family." The crossbreeding between American and European grapes is what makes growing *vinifera* possible in the United States. Muscadine grapes, like Virginia's norton, grow naturally and are not subject to the same pests and diseases that make nonnative grapes impossible to grow without intervention.

Although the wines produced in the Southeast have a deep history, there have been problems getting restaurants and consumers to accept them as legitimate wines. Mary Ann, of Persimmon Creek Vineyards in Georgia, describes her first cold call sales attempt, in 2003, at a restaurant named Georgia's in the Ritz Carlton Greensboro in North Carolina:

> He refused to taste them because they were from Georgia.
> ... What grows together goes together. If you're going to have local Southern foods then why not offer some beverage that is quality and that is good from your place? ... If you're from Georgia and you say, "I've never had a Georgia wine," then I say to you, "Go and taste your dirt. Try it. Taste your place."

Although she was unsuccessful at the time, the restaurant came back several months later and agreed to put the wine on its menu, after which a restaurant in the Ritz Carlton Miami sought out her wines. Unfortunately, she is unable to sell them in Florida due to distribution laws that restrict the sale of alcoholic beverages between states (Pennell, 2017).

The current success of North Carolina and Georgia wineries is in part linked to the success of the local food movement. Consumers' desire for nonindustrially produced goods extends beyond food to include beverages as well. Mary Ann explains that although initially it is easier to separate the liquid appearing in a wine glass from its agricultural origins than it is to separate vegetables from their farm origins, this should not be the case:

> Wine is agricultural, and people forget that. In restaurants you walk in and you see glasses, and it's not like squash, it's not like asparagus; it's not something you can actually touch. ... bottles [do] not grow on the vine. ... Whenever you see bottles you should really see a vineyard; you should see earth.

The connection between the earth and the final product, or the sense of terroir, was frequently mentioned by winery owners as integral to their experience working through the wine making process, because the success of a varietal and the subsequent taste will vary based on the weather each year and the specific location where the vines are planted. Although the first image to come to mind when discussing tasting a place is a farmers' market or farm-to-table restaurant, wine, beer, and spirits are slowly becoming a dominant player in that sphere, with local wineries and breweries setting up stands alongside local bakeries and farmers at neighborhood farmers' markets. This connection to place and the land can also be seen in the family histories of winemaking and farming.

Family history

Although winemaking on a commercial scale, post-Prohibition, only dates back to the 1970s in the Southeast, there is a deep history of alcohol production that goes back generations. Among the most stereotypical forms of alcohol production in the region is moonshine and the bootlegging that went along with it (Lippard and Stewart, 2019). However, moonshine was not the only form of alcohol produced in homes throughout the South. Bo explains how his family's history intersected around wine, moonshine, and bootlegging after his grandfather obtained a liquor-making license during Prohibition:

> He decided that he'd make it for the government, but he didn't want to lose his other business, so he started making wine. And the people that bought a whole lot of liquor, he always said they needed a Christmas present so he made blueberry and muscadine wine. ... That's the reason I like to make blueberry wine; it just reminds me of being a teenager at home when it was being made there.

His family has a history of bootlegging going back more than 250 years, and as a young man he ran liquor. When moonshine was legalized, one of his uncles was the first person in North Carolina to get a license. Today, Bo uses his family's history to shape his winemaking recipes at his Garden Gate Winery in North Carolina. However, the admitted purposes for drinking wine have changed somewhat. Bo continues: "When I was a kid my grandpa would make blackberry wine, and if we had an upset stomach my grandma would make us drink a glass. But back then wine was used as a medicine." A reliance on family experience was not uncommon, especially for wineries producing fruit or muscadine wine, both of which grow with little intervention in the South.

Bob explains how his family started making wine long before they opened Hinnant Family Vineyards as a commercial winery in North Carolina:

> I remember [Willard] and my uncle Glen, they made wine for 20 years, so we had some background in it. And

the rest we learned on the job, along with assistance from other winemakers in Florida and Arkansas. ... But there's a learning curve there. It seems like with every year we get better at it.

While some families had experience with homemade wine, others sought out the expertise of other winemakers, especially during the early years of Southern wine, because there was limited information coming from official sources such as local universities. Echoing Gabriele's frustration with Virginia Tech's refusal to support his early winemaking endeavors at Barboursville, Charles, from Still Pond Winery in Georgia, explains how it was difficult to find information when starting his venture:

It was not a lot of information through the University of Georgia. Nobody else here in the state was doing it at that time. Got a lot of information out of the Carolinas, mainly North Carolina; South Carolina had a few small vineyards going in, but it was lot of trial and error to begin with.

He explains how his father decided which types of muscadine grapes to plant, in the mid-to late 1960s, when there were no grapes planted in the area. Some of the earliest winery owners, including Lillian of Westbend Winery in North Carolina, continue to take pride in their ability to help other wineries get started: "We, back in the early days, helped a lot of people get started in this business, because at that time, there wasn't anywhere else for them to go. ... Now there are lots of organizations out there to help prospective vineyard owners, but it wasn't that way in the beginning." Although institutional support has developed, with numerous universities offering extension support as well as viticulture majors, the strength of community ties between winemakers continues to shape the Southern wine industry.

As growing grapes for winemaking slowly became an accepted agricultural venture, other winery owners were able to seek out advice from their state agriculture departments. Dave explains how his father started growing muscadine grapes:

[My father] contacted the North Carolina Department of Agriculture and said, "What's the best crop to plant?" And back then there was a big winery out of New York paying $350 per ton for our native muscadine grapes. ... In those four years the price fell from $350 to $125 a ton, and we were stuck with a whole bunch of grapes. We like to say that we're Methodists because we couldn't be Baptists; we had to get into the wine business and find a market for our grapes.

His family and several others in the North Carolina area started growing muscadine grapes in 1968 when there was high demand from wineries in New York. However, the state department of agriculture's encouragement to plant muscadine grapes led to the flooding of the market and plummeting prices, leaving owners facing the conundrum of how to make a profit off their grapes. The solution for Dave's family was to start making their own wine instead of relying on selling their grapes to wineries outside the state.

Other wineries that started more recently were able to seek out the expertise of universities with dedicated viticulture programs, such as Virginia Tech. Lenna from RagApple Lassie Vineyards, located in the North Carolina piedmont, explains:

> A professor at Virginia Tech stated to someone in this area, he said, "I'm sure you all can grow French *vinifera* grapes down there because they are doing well in Virginia." ... Prior to that time, all the energies in North Carolina and from NC State [University], which is our land grant university, had been directed toward muscadine. ... So with that little push, it just somehow took root and went from one French *vinifera* winery to today there are 22 inside the Yadkin Valley appellation. ... All this has happened since 1999.

Although North Carolina has a large number of muscadine-centric vineyards, especially around the coast where Duplin is located, the Yadkin Valley, on the opposite side of the state in the piedmont, has become known for *vinifera* grapes in the same way most Virginia wineries are known for theirs.

The wineries also represent family businesses with multiple generations working together. Charles explains how his father's desire to plant grapes started a multigenerational family business: "My father was the general manager for the cattle operation and was responsible for the initial planting of the grapes ... we're a whole family here now. Both of my sons work here. My youngest son is the winemaker; my oldest son is the vineyard manager." His son chimes in: "I went to Valdosta State University and got a degree in marketing. ... I always knew I wanted to come back here. At that point we were in a transition phase. We were in fresh fruit and knew we had to do something else in order to survive." Shortly after he returned to the farm following graduation, the winery opened its tasting room and started selling wine.

Other wineries are still run by first-generation owners, but they hope their children will carry on the business. Lenna, from RagApple Lassie Vineyards, explains that although she and her husband are running the winery, they hope that "our children will carry on the vineyard; they have great pride in that. ... As to the rest of the farming, no. We're counting on having everything established firmly enough that growing corn, wheat, and soybeans will not be a necessity for them." Wineries offer an alternative to traditional farming practices for the next generation as they did for tobacco and apple farmers in the late 1990s and early 2000s, when agricultural prices for those crops declined (Carter, 2013).

While some families have a history of alcohol production and distribution, the desire to see the next generation carry it on changes when it is no longer an illegal enterprise. Bo notes: "I think I would like to see one of my kids to do it, but the basic fact, it's been in the family all these years, and now it's legal and I'd just like to see my kids carry it out." Bo's family has a history of bootlegging and making moonshine, and his early experiences around liquor were as a bootlegger, but today he hopes his children will carry on Garden Gate Winery.

These family-run wineries also set the space for consumers to return to the land, offering a connection to the land and agriculture that has disappeared for most modern families. Felicia, of Oakencroft Winery, explains:

> There's a new word that's been coined, agrotourism, in which—it was never when I started the vineyard here, and agrotours are—is visiting farms, but particularly wineries where the grapes are grown here on the—under the Farm Winery License. ... It's like we're hopefully becoming the Napa Valley of the East.

Agrotourism facilitates the connection between people and the land while allowing the industries traditionally grounded in agriculture to flourish.

While some wineries sell their wine to tourists and visitors, others have U-pick operations as well that allow guests to get out into the vineyard and pick grapes. Bob tries to connect consumers to the farm through his U-pick program: "Tourism—Ag tourism, you know. People love the—the farms are gone. I mean, if you look around, everybody lives on concrete and asphalt, and they just love to get out in a vineyard and walk around." Hinnant Family Vineyards goes a step further and hosts an event where people who previously came and picked grapes for their own homemade wine are invited back to the vineyard. Bob continues: "We do a festival every year in the spring; it's called the Local Yokel Sip-Off, and it's just for those home winemakers. They bring their wines back in and we get a judge from NC State [University] to come in and judge them and we give out awards." The connection between family-run businesses and the community allows these spaces to be tourist destinations while also maintaining a connection to the local community through various events. Although wineries' premier purpose is to sell wine, most have family-friendly events such as concerts and barbecues that allow parents to imbibe while their children are entertained (Pennell, 2017). Yet, in all these instances, there remains a connection to the land that is too often romanticized.

Farm wine

Winery tasting rooms offer consumers a chance to connect with the farm and relax, away from the stress of daily life, but as with restaurants whose relaxing dining rooms and elegant service put diners at ease, both hide the hardships of extreme temperatures, work accidents, and hard labor that go into producing the finished products consumers enjoy (Fine, 1996; Pennell, 2017). Wineries tap into the agricultural history of the South in two main ways. They can be a solution to existing financial trouble as commodity crop prices fall, but they bring their own financial risks because they are still subject to variations in the weather.

Wineries, like all agricultural production endeavors, struggle with the weather; too much rain or extreme temperatures at the wrong time can reduce the yield of a crop as well as change the taste of the wine. Lillian describes her experiences with a commercial winery:

> Wineries and vineyards are wonderful, but they can be black holes when it comes to throwing money in them, and so it became a passion. ... We have weather irregularities here, such as spring frosts where you lose all of the—the first year we were a commercial winery, we lost 80 percent of our crop because we had this late spring frost in mid-May—unheard of. ... It's farming is what it is, so you have to deal with the weather.

The late spring frost froze the early buds, decimating the crop for that year, as it did again in May 2020 when a late frost decimated a majority of the early budding vines across the South. While some wineries are able to install fan systems that prevent the frost from settling on the vines, those systems are expensive and are out of reach for a majority of the vineyards in the region.

Other wineries, especially those along the coast, have to deal with hurricanes, as the extreme wind and heavy rain can destroy the plants, but too much rain also impacts the taste of the finished product. Bo, from Hinnant Family Vineyards, stresses that although wineries have been romanticized, they are still agricultural endeavors:

> There's no romance in this. People get this romantic idea but it's all work, a lot of hours, lot of deadlines, lot of bad things like hurricanes. ... Ten years ago, I think you'd have 500 plants in a field that knocked over in one night when Fran came through. ... So if we can just make it to the end of September without a hurricane, we're good.

Wineries along the North Carolina coast, where most muscadine grapes are grown, are especially vulnerable to hurricanes.

Despite the problems caused by freezing temperatures and excessive rains, wineries can also be a solution for struggling farmers. Willard explains his decision to plant grape vines for what became Hinnant Family Vineyards: "My family were farmers, tobacco farmers, cotton mainly, a little bit of corn and soybeans in those days. When I inherited the farm, we had a small tobacco allotment, and one reason we went into grapes was to increase the income from the farm." The extra income from selling grapes made it possible to keep the farm in the family for at least another generation. Without transitioning to include grapes, it was unlikely the farm could be maintained as prices fell.

While it is easy for a consumer to get caught up in the tasting room and trappings offered by wineries, there is extensive backstage work going on. Sociologist Erving Goffman (1959) explains that businesses, like restaurants, are split into the front stage and backstage. The front stage is the version customers see, while the backstage is where the work takes place. Wineries are a prime example of the balance between front and backstage. The backstage takes place out in the vineyard or in the bottling room, away from the eyes of customers; while this makes it possible to enjoy the finished product without much thought for what goes into it, it also reinforces wineries' place in consumer culture as an escape from the harsh realities of daily life (Pennell, 2017).

Wineries are selling not only a product but also the space and the experience; many have become major tourist destinations, hosting weddings and events on a regular basis as well as large yearly festivals. Some wineries rely on their proximity to other attractions, such as Myrtle Beach. Dave explains:

> Last year we had 82,000 visitors. ... We are a day trip from most major cities. ... But also, North Carolina has such pristine and beautiful beaches. ... I think we estimated there were nine million tourists that visited our beaches this year, and we work very hard at trying to let them know that it doesn't rain at Duplin Wine Cellars when it's raining at the beach.

Wineries offer an alternative to a rainy day by the water while also allowing people to connect with local businesses and agriculture. Other vineyards are part of a long history of agricultural innovation. Jerry explains how the winery was the logical next step to preserve the agricultural history of the Biltmore property in Asheville, North Carolina as well as to combat the impact of gas shortages on tourism in the late 1970s.

> We had gas shortages that summer [1979] ... the tourist business had been really important from 1970 on and still is. But it was driving the profitability of the estate ... and Mr. Cecil felt really uncomfortable having somebody in the Middle East being able to turn off the tap and drive his business south. So he was looking for an alternative and became fixated with wine as a solution. ... The agriculture history of the estate has been a tradition since Mr. Vanderbilt started. ... The tourists were great, but it's an 8,000 acre working farm. ... We put in a little over 200 acres of *vinifera*, which we were really the first major *vinifera* grower on the East Coast.

Wineries' proximity to other tourist attractions also helps facilitate their success. The Biltmore winery is only one aspect of a large tourist destination that includes house and garden tours as well as restaurants. Visitors can spend days touring the entire property and stop by the tasting room all in one easy trip. The success of wineries as community and tourist destinations helps justify the costly decision to open a winery, even when accounting for the financial risk involved in growing grapes.

Although farm wineries are considered agricultural in nature, in Virginia they are also governed by the Virginia Alcoholic Beverage Control Authority (VA ABC), which defines the proportions of estate-grown grapes required to be labeled a Virginia wine. The Class A farm winery license requires that at least 51 percent of the grapes or agricultural product (these laws also apply to cider) used to make wine must be grown on the farm and no more than 25 percent may be grown outside the state. The Class B license requires 75 percent of the grapes to be grown in the state and no more than 25 percent to be grown outside the state (VA ABC, 2020). The Class B category allows a winemaker to buy grapes from farmers, while the Class A category requires the winemaker to grow their own grapes. Historically most winemakers grew a majority of their own grapes, but it is becoming more common to buy grapes due to the limited availability and prohibitive price of land.

Aside from directly asking the winemaker about the provenance of the grapes, a consumer can look at the wine label to get more information about the origins of the grapes. The phrase "bottled by" only refers to where the wine was bottled and is most commonly used when the grapes were not grown by the winery. The label "produced and bottled by" refers to the making of the wine; although typically the grapes are grown on the winery's property, it can also apply to grapes that were purchased but processed on site. The phrase "grown, produced, and bottled by" means almost all the grapes in that wine were grown on the property where the wine was produced and then bottled. The phrase "estate grown," often appearing on the front label, means the winery is located in an established AVA and almost all the grapes were grown on the property (DuCard Vineyards, ND). These distinctions make it possible for Virginia wineries to buy grapes when necessary while still making these sourcing differences visible to the consumer who is aware of what these phrases signal.

While Virginia has taken steps to control what wine can be called Virginia wine and set the bar at a minimum of 51 percent state-grown grapes, other states have more flexible bars. North Carolina, for example, sets the minimum at 5 percent state-grown grapes (NC Wine, 2020). In Georgia, wineries in the Dahlongea Plateau, Georgia's only AVA, must grow at least 85 percent of the grapes on their property to use the AVA designation (WSB-TV, 2018). The various minimums for the percentage of grapes grown on site make it difficult for consumers to know exactly where the grapes in their glass are coming from and increase competition within wine markets.

Wine markets

Starting a winery is an expensive endeavor, from the cost of land and grapes to building a tasting room and purchasing all the necessary equipment to make, store, and bottle wine. While wineries are inherently agricultural in nature, there is a large market for wine, and yet the wineries in the Southeast are only minor players in the country's market, with the California wine industry being the industry leader. Although Virginia does have the seventh largest number of wineries, with 307 as of 2018 (North Carolina is tenth with 175 wineries), California alone has 4,613 wineries (Conway, 2020). Thus, the Southeastern wineries remain a small player in the US wine market.

Although Southeastern wine has a longer history than wines in California, they are still relatively young in the current winemaking scene. However, California's success lends credibility to Virginia varietals: "California has a respect of being a wine-growing state, and now they are getting involved in viognier and petit manseng and tannat ... they add credibility to those particular varietals. ... They are doing it very successfully and it adds credibility to the marketplace." Dennis explains that viognier, petit manseng, and tannat are three of the grapes Virginia wineries claim but historically were not prevalent in the California wine scene but are becoming increasingly popular on both coasts.

Although California is a dominant player in the international wine scene, it was not until the 1970s, when California wines beat French wines in a blind taste test, specifically the Judgement of Paris in 1976 orchestrated by world-renowned wine expert Steve Spurrier, that the emerging US wine industry began to be recognized as a major presence in the international wine market (Robinson and Murphy, 2013). Jerry, from Biltmore Winery, explains the benefits of the changing wine scene:

> If you went to New York in 1971 and went to the best restaurant and asked for the wine list, you wouldn't see any California wines on there. It was all French wines. ... The development of California being perceived as fine wine is relatively late occurring, and that's the beauty of emerging markets like North Carolina.

While it is still somewhat unusual to find a Southeastern wine on the most exclusive wine lists, the quality of the wine in the region is improving dramatically and restaurants in New York City and Chicago do feature Barboursville wines (Carter, 2013).

Despite this increased success, local wineries are still struggling to claim a larger share of the wine market. While competition among wineries is not uncommon, winery owners also work together toward their shared goals. One way of doing this is through wine trails, where wineries within the same region will partner together to create tourism packets featuring information from all the partnered wineries. Lillian explains how other winemakers see the establishment of AVAs as another step toward establishing credibility:

> The terroir is your soil, your weather, your—what makes this place unique, and North Carolina is very agriculturally ... I don't think we want to be compared with California, which we all know is the Garden of Eden. ... Here our wines reflect the vintage year, the growing, and the terroir. ... I think our terroir, with the soil reflecting the quality of fruity and the weather conditions, I think it's good. I mean, otherwise we wouldn't have been granted our AVA, our American Viticultural Area designation, back in, I believe it was 2003—gave great credibility to our region.

These AVAs and wine trails offer consumers a way to discover new wineries and wine regions they may otherwise not be familiar with. Other less official ways of supporting nearby wineries is by recommending that customers visit specific ones. Chris, from Pearmund Winery, explains how he bridges camaraderie with the desire for a larger market share among Virginia wineries:

> Of all the wine sold in Virginia, 4 percent is Virginia wine. That's basically one out of every 25 bottles purchased in Virginia is a Virginia wine product. We're kind of competing against the rest of the wine world. ... So if we can communicate well to share our knowledge to reduce problems, to cooperatively use our purchasing power as a single entity ... by using the same supplier we get the same price as Kendall Jackson.

He explains that purchasing in bulk has lowered the price of wine barrels as well, helping to reduce the cost and benefiting everyone who is willing to work together. The need to collaborate is in part a result of the high financial demands of running a winery. Like restaurants, it is not only about the taste of the finished product; it is the entire experience surrounding a customer, and for wineries cultivating that experience is expensive, as Chris continues to explain:

> We're not selling glasses and bottles of wine anymore. We're selling ambiance, we're selling a place in time, we're selling an environment. ... We can only survive on better quality, more expensive wines, and more expensive environments. To create a winery near Washington, DC, Northern Virginia is also expensive land. You can be spending $30,000, $40,000, $50,000 an acre for agriculture land and another $20,000 to $25,000 to plant a decent vineyard, and $1,000,000 to $2,000,000 to build a winery.

Although the cost of starting a winery varies based on the cost of land in an area, the desire to sell an experience as well as a finished product continually shapes the decisions of winemakers, including the type of grapes to grow and the type of experience you want a customer to have when they enter the tasting room.

The decision regarding what type of grapes to grow and which wines to make reflects an understanding of what can grow in the region, what the consumers desire, and where a specific winery fits in the larger market. Jerry explains the decision to focus on *vinifera* grapes:

> It really wasn't about making North Carolina wine. It was about making Biltmore wine and that if we were going to be successful in the broad competition of wines, we had to compete with French wines, we have to compete with California wine. ... That's who we were fighting for space on the shelf.

While some winemakers see California as competition, others credit the state with introducing consumers to wine. Dennis from Horton Winery, located less than one and a half miles from Barboursville Vineyards in Virginia, explains the relationship between California wines and the success of his fruit wines: "I think we all ought to send a check to Sutter Home. They made the first semi-sweet or sweet, blush, and what did that do? That probably introduced millions and millions of people to the wine industry because it was very acceptable to almost everybody's palate." While he continues that most people will follow a progression of wine starting with the sweeter wines and slowly progressing to drier whites and eventually reds, his fruit wines enjoy a steady popularity among customers.

Although most vineyards' goal is to produce their own wines, many start out by selling their grapes to other winemakers who are unable to grow the number of grapes they need for production. Willard describes the early days of Hinnant Family Vineyards: "We basically tried to package and sell all we could fresh, because that was a lot more money in it than it was selling to a winery. But whatever we had left we always sold to the wineries. And mainly Duplin because we were actually stockholders in Duplin." This goes back to the early days of the muscadine wineries in North Carolina, when Duplin needed grapes and did not have the money to buy them while other vineyards needed to sell their grapes. Thus, Duplin traded stock in their winery for grapes. This system gave the vineyards a stable customer for their grapes and gave Duplin a stable supply of grapes so they could meet the increasing consumer demand for muscadine wine.

Although a small player on the international wine market, the success of Southeastern wineries in attracting consumers seeking out a taste of place either where they live or on their travels has made wineries an attractive business option for those interested in winemaking. This success has created the necessary support system that was lacking when the first wineries began opening in the 1970s. Now winemakers can seek assistance from institutionalized sources such as local universities and extension agents, as well as from other winemakers in the region who are more experienced. Yet the success of becoming a community oriented industry is not without its own internal problems, especially in terms of race and gender inequities.

Inequality in the vineyard

Although wineries offer consumers an escape from reality, behind the scenes they are subject to the same inequalities impacting the rest of society, ranging from a lack of women winemakers and owners to immigration and labor debates. Mary Ann, from Persimmon Creek Vineyards, explains the history of the Georgia land her winery sits on today:

> I admire that in a woman because it is so much harder. She was a beautiful woman and she could outrun the revenuers. ... She was respected not just because she was [making liquor] but what she did and could do. She was driven by

eking out a livelihood for herself and her kids. So she grew corn and made bootleg.

Here, Mary Ann notes her regard for the woman who ran the now abandoned still on the winery and raised corn where the grapes grow today. She was a single mother during a time when there was no grocery store, so she found a way to make a living for herself, and she serves as a point of pride and inspiration for the current winery owner who makes a living from the same land, albeit in a legal way.

Other winemakers point to the few women winemakers in their states as evidence of continuing inequality in the industry. Although Felicia ran her winery the entire time it was open, she sees a dearth of other female-headed wineries: "There's a single woman up in Middleburg, but they're few and far between. They are mostly families—couples where the wife is helping with the husband, but I can't think of many wineries where there's just a single woman operating without having a male partner." The one well-known exception is the woman who runs a vineyard in Loudon County, Virginia, who is transgender. However, although the owner has been the topic of recent discussion, including in *The Wild Vine* by Todd Kilman (2011), which focuses on the history of the norton grape and the owner Jenni McCloud's championing of the grape, there is nothing at the winery other than the image of a butterfly transforming on the main label to connect the final product with the owner's personal story. Women winemakers, while becoming more common across the world, are still underrepresented in the profession. As Ann Matasar (2006) found in her work on women in the wine industry, there is an emphasis on passion for wine, which is often seen as critical for the focus and self-confidence that is needed to have a successful career despite numerous challenges, including limited access to the necessary financial capital compared with their male counterparts.

Wineries are considered agricultural endeavors and as such are subject to the same labor laws. Dennis explains the problems his winery has had finding workers, even though a majority of the workers in the vineyard are from Mexico and return to his vineyard every year, many having done so for more than a decade:

> With all the political baloney that's going on, we belong to the H-2A Program [agricultural guest worker program], and under that we basically have to hire every American that applies. And we do, of which there have been two, and right now I think I've got 23 hands in the vineyard. So

without the Mexican market ... nobody wants to work for eight, ten, or 13 dollars an hour working in the vineyard when they can flip hamburgers for nine dollars.

Labor issues in agriculture are not a new topic of discussion, as the mistreatment of migrant workers has long been a concern in the South and in the wine industry. Journalist Barry Estabrook chronicles the slave-like conditions and vulnerability of tomato farm workers in Florida, for example. Although the success of the Coalition of Immokalee Workers has helped improve working conditions, there is still a long way to go in protecting agricultural laborers (Estabrook, 2011). Similarly, journalist Tracie McMillan investigates the grape industry specifically, where workers are not protected by agriculture laws and are not given a lunch break (although California has implemented a 30-minute break in a nine-hour day and one day off per week for agricultural workers), there are no federal protections, and most states do not provide a minimum wage or overtime pay for agricultural workers, nor do child labor laws apply to agricultural workers (McMillan, 2012). Not all wineries rely on migrant labor to maintain and pick their grapes; some use volunteers and others employ local high school and college students. That said, it is not uncommon to drive by a vineyard during the summer and see a group of Latinos working along the vines.

While many winery owners do not mention labor or gender as a factor in their experience, several have faced issues within their local community because they are producing alcohol, which reflects the conservative and evangelical cultural contours of the region. Lenna discusses the problem some family and community members have with her family's North Carolina winery:

> This is a rural community. We're right in the heart of the Bible Belt, and Frank actually had three or four people, including an uncle, show up at the store and tell him his soul was being endangered, if he proceeded to plant a vineyard and make wine. ... We probably have neighbors that we can see their homes from here, who have never been in the doors here, but it's amazing how many people come up to us when we're in the community and tell us they are proud of the tourism capabilities and what's happening in Yadkin County, and that it is helping provide other streams of revenue for Yadkin County.

Although Prohibition ended nearly 100 years ago, there are still several dry counties throughout the South, and even in counties that allow the sale of liquor there is still a strong religious contingent that does not look favorably on alcohol consumption. This makes it difficult for farmers-turned-winemakers who see wine as a necessary step to saving their family's land and agricultural history to find support among members of their local community. In many cases these wineries rely on the support of tourists passing through the area instead of their neighbors for their financial success.

Conclusion

Winemakers are engaging in the process of fabricating an authentic craft product by focusing on the place-based quality, the terroir, that is unique to their land to market the product to customers within their community as well as tourists looking to take a piece of the South home with them (Peterson, 1997). The careful separation between the front and backstage of winemaking endeavors allows consumers to literally buy into the romanticism of sipping a glass of wine in an elegant tasting room or on a beautiful outdoor patio overlooking the rolling hills, while behind a sliding door and down a spiral staircase, out of sight and out of mind, lies the production center where winemakers carefully monitor the fermentation and aging process that transforms grapes into wine, and migrant workers are on the far side of the vineyard tending to the vines, also out of sight and mind for patrons of the winery. All this is an intricate balance of impression management: selling the recovery of the long-lost winemaking tradition of the region and removing from visibility the inequality and struggle involved in producing the elegant wines consumers buy to provide a getaway from everyday life (Fine, 1996).

Although winemaking is not new to the Southeast, the wine industry's reputation as a legitimate producer of wine in a country long dominated by California's wine industry shows not only the increasing demand for local products, but also the desire among consumers to seek out these authentic experiences that are grounded in the agricultural traditions of the region. Farmers are also able to transition away from historical cash crops such as tobacco to more modern endeavors that are not only marketable to large industries but can be sold directly to consumers via tasting rooms and restaurants. The resilience of Southern farmers to tap into the rising demand for craft or authentic products by buying into the growing wine industry has helped many families hold onto their land in spite of decreasing agricultural revenues.

2

Water and Waves: The Rebirth of Coastal Fishing Communities

Blue crabs from the Chesapeake Bay spiced with Old Bay seasoning. Fresh shrimp off the coast of Louisiana dropped off in kitchens across the bayous and into the heart of New Orleans. Rockfish, porgy, crawfish, and spot, among many other varieties of seafood, are central to the heartbeat of food culture along the coastlines of the South. The commercial fishing industry across the southeastern United States offers an in-depth look into the connection between the current local and craft food movement and the harsh reality of continually operating a business that's livelihood is vulnerable to natural and human disasters. Yet the resiliency embedded in this industry strengthens the social solidarity within these communities that line the Atlantic Ocean and Gulf Coast, similar to the social networks that exist between producers and consumers in the craft beer industry, allowing these businesses to thrive despite pushback from other sources (Borer, 2019). While restaurant chefs are able to highlight their dedication to local seafood through their menus and the self-selecting clientele who are seeking out the associated status conveyed upon those who choose to eat local (Johnston and Baumann, 2010), in this relationship the chef is often the center of attention from both the diner and the media. However, their success is dependent on their suppliers, in this case the fishermen and women who endure hurricanes, oil spills, and various forms of government regulation to provide their customers and local chefs with fresh seafood while also continuing to operate their family businesses, which in many cases have been in operation for multiple generations.

Most of the people watching the Food Network, one of the top 25 television channels in 2019 (Schneider, 2019), or one of the other networks featuring cooking shows, such as Bravo's Emmy award-winning *Top Chef* (the network places just behind the Food Network in popularity), are unlikely to ever see the people responsible for seafood production, with few exceptions. *Top Chef* does highlight commercial fishing or some form of procuring seafood from the water in several seasons, including sea urchin or uni in Santa Barbara, fishing off Montauk, New York, oysters in Seattle, and shrimp each time *Top Chef* has been filmed in the South—in New Orleans and Charleston. Highlighting the importance of the fishing communities in these popular television shows provides a window into how important these industries are in the coastal South.

Top Chef filmed in New Orleans in 2013, eight years after Hurricane Katrina and three years after the Deepwater Horizon oil spill (often referred to as the "BP oil spill" because the oil rig was owned by BP). The tourism department used funds from the oil relief program to sponsor the show; this was the first time commercial fishing was featured on the show in a way that highlighted not only the process of procuring seafood, but also the people who are integral to the industry. Eddie Huang, a popular chef, discusses the influx of Vietnamese immigrants and refugees into the region: "Around the 1970s, tens of thousands of Vietnamese came to New Orleans and really invested their time, their sweat, and their energy into the shrimping industry." The cheftestants go to the shrimping dock and watch how the shrimp are sucked out from the hull of the boat, then weighed and put on ice, as one of the dockworkers describes the operations of the docks since their opening in 1973. What makes this unique is that, across the television series, this episode is the only one to present producers of seafood who are not white men and women.

Years later, *Top Chef* filmed in Charleston, South Carolina, in spring 2016. In the second episode of the season, the cheftestants were treated to a low country boil by one of Charleston's leading chefs, Frank Lee. After dumping the Old Bay-seasoned, steaming-hot shrimp, sausage, potatoes, and corn onto a sheet of brown butcher paper covering an old picnic table, Lee explains what they are going to eat: "What we have here is a low country boil. The shrimp came out of our water just an hour ago." Tom Colicchio, the head judge of the show and an award-winning chef, describes the changes he has witnessed in the Charleston food scene: "Twenty years ago, when I first started coming down here, a lot of the local chefs really weren't using this local stuff; you [Frank Lee] really started that tradition, and it's great to see so many young chefs following." Although the chefs do not see the process of shrimping in the local waters in this episode, several episodes later viewers are provided with a brief snapshot of the cheftestants going out on a shrimping boat.

When the cheftestants head out on the shrimping boat, Tom Colicchio describes what the they are going to do: "This is Captain Tommy; he is going to take us out shrimping." The captain and a black deckhand pull up the shrimp net, dumping out a net full of shrimp as well as other fishing byproducts, and the chefs are told to "pick everything out that looks edible and then let the rest of it go," while a pelican sits in the background waiting for them to discard the bycatch. Then, as one of the chefs picks through the shrimp, the captain explains: "Carolina shrimp have a very unique flavor because they come out of this warm water, but they are still very firm and have a very sweet texture; it is just really plump, juicy, flavorful shrimp." This fishing trip ends with the cheftestants competing on the dock of a Charleston restaurant known for its freshly sourced seafood.

Locally sourcing seafood is now a hallmark of many chefs across urban areas hoping to tap into the local food movement and consumer demand for craft, locally sourced products that are seen as embedded with more authenticity than their industrially produced counterparts (Johnston and Baumann, 2010). However, the attention is firmly placed on the chefs who serve food directly to the consumers, not on the producers responsible for the cultivation of these products. The trials and tribulations of the commercial fishermen and women responsible for keeping chefs supplied with the local seafood their customers demand are largely ignored as doting customers focus on the plates placed in front of them, eager to snap pictures for their Instagram pages, and the chefs who use the seafood, ultimately missing the important role these community members play in cultivating the local food movement ingredients customers demand. This reinforces the need to expand the definition of craft products and their producers beyond just handcrafted finished goods, to include the raw materials that go into those finished products, in this case the people responsible for catching fresh seafood.

From hurricanes to oil spills, the coastal South must cope with many difficulties in depending on the sea for their livelihood. Within these communities scattered across the bayous, inlets, and barrier islands of the Gulf of Mexico and Atlantic Ocean are engrained food traditions and knowledge emphasizing the importance of the sea and its provision for families and Southern foodways. Yet these communities' existence is tenuous due to past tragedies that continue to impact the lives of the fishing communities and restaurant owners long after the devastation has faded from national headlines. The success of these communities is often dependent on chefs and consumers in major urban areas demanding local or regional products and being willing to pay for them instead of buying cheaper, foreign-produced alternatives. This chapter poses the question: how does an industry so vulnerable to changes in the environment, consumer demand, and government policy continue to sustain itself in today's modern economy?

The fishing profession

Unlike the winemakers who turned to wine as a way to maintain their family farms and agricultural traditions, the men and women who make their living on the water are often the next generation in a long line of family fishing traditions. Most fishermen and women are not new to the industry, as many learned from watching their parents make a living on the water at a very young age. Randy started helping his father in the water off the North Carolina coast when he was seven years old: "I used to go bay scalloping every Monday and Wednesday and I never went to school until 11 o'clock that day 'cause I went with Daddy scalloping that morning. And I went to school at 11 o'clock so I wouldn't be counted absent that day." Randy knew at a young age that he wanted to continue working on the water, and instead of prioritizing school he helped his father on the water so that one day he could take over the business. Pierre, of Louisiana, bought his first boat at age 12 and started shrimping on his own, which he credits his father for teaching him: "My daddy trained us right to make a living on the land, and he trained us how not to be dangerous, and he trusted us enough that he pretty much let us do that. Because that was our way of life." Like Randy, Pierre knew from an early age that he was going to be a commercial fisherman; it was a way of life, one that he maintains despite the risks involved.

Although many children from fishing families follow in their parents' footsteps, others choose a different route. Ira describes his experience as a child, in a coastal North Carolina town, before the invention of outboard motors: "Most everybody worked in the water. I dug clams out there or picked buckets, rolling off for seven cents a pail." He was exposed to the Coast Guard as a child and dreamed about joining as an adult. After several friends and family members joined the military in the late 1920s and early 1930s, he saw it as a steady form of employment that was otherwise unavailable on the island, and in 1938 he enlisted. He explains why he left the fishing industry for a career in the Coast Guard:

> I come home that night and told Papa, "Papa, I ain't doing it no more." Father did this all his life and now

he's—retirement age, no benefits. I said, "Papa, you worked all your life on that water and all you got to show for it is two empty hands. You expect me to do the same. No, something better than this. I'm going."

The desire for stable employment and benefits drives some children away from the fishing industry into the military or toward factory work.

The balance between a love of the water and a desire to continue in the fishing industry poses a challenge for the next generation of fishing families. When asked if any of his children intend to follow in his footsteps and fish off the coast of South Carolina, Fred says:

What the work means, I think, is passed down to all three of them. But will any of them do it? I don't know. I really think that to fish you have to want to do nothing but that. There are easier ways to make money. ... You have to really like the whole package so much you don't mind the downside.

Fred's children, while understanding the value of the hard work fishing entails, remain undecided if they are going to join their father in the business.

Other parents have watched their children seek out a life on the water as an alternative to other forms of employment. Jan explains how she and her husband used to go clamming along the North Carolina coast during the summers for fun. Today, it has also become a path of employment for several of her children who chose not to go to college:

We have enjoyed [clamming]. It has been lucrative for some of our younger boys that wanted to go and do that for a living. It's a hard living but if they didn't want to go to school and get an education, they did what they could to make a living out of the water.

Despite the difficulties involved in making a life from the sea, there are still people willing to do it, and for many it is a viable alternative to college. David explains that one of the newest members of his South Carolina-based crew comes from a family of lawyers, but he chose to go into commercial fishing: "His father, I'm sure, is mortified because they're all lawyers and he is very much not a lawyer. ... It's kind of a changing of the guard because of all the regulations, so you're seeing a lot of dudes that were in it getting out." Although there has been a decrease in the number of commercial fishermen, he continues:

> I think it's a viable thing. I don't think you are supposed to eat your fish out of a net from anywhere. I think you're supposed to be eating them right here. Somebody has got to feed the lawyers and doctors snapper and grouper when they go out to eat. ... That's the little people.

As David notes, the demand for seafood ensures there will always be a need for commercial fishermen, but it is not always about seeking an alternative to higher education. Indeed, as the consumption of and demand for seafood increases, there will be greater opportunities for fishermen to sell their products (Kerns, 2020)

Frank explains that although a lot of the older fisherman in his Mississippi community are retiring or just getting out of the business, he sees hope for the next generation in the industry coming from an unlikely source:

> It used to be, well, you've seen the movie *Forrest Gump*? But now, with *The Deadliest Catch* and things like this, where they actually put commercial fishing in the house, all across the world, I guess it's just allure that people see that, and there's still this sense of adventure and they're just striking out to get your fortune.

The risks and adventure built into a life on the water are appealing for a new generation whose exposure to commercial fishing comes from the glitz of a reality television show. As Frank mentions, the newcomers are not local, and as a result they are not becoming part of the community in the same way fishermen were previously. Jamie explains: "Well, the people I'm seeing coming into it, I can't really say their ages because it's not really no local people that's getting into it. It's people that's moving from other cities." He is one of the youngest oystermen in the South Carolina area, at 35, but the business has been in his family for almost 75 years. Those in the oyster industry that he sees coming from other cities often collect oysters and then return to their own cities to sell them. Like the motivations behind the craft food industry in New York City, many Southern fishermen and women would feel out of place in the white-collar workplace, and in reality, unlike in urban areas where white-collar work is easily found, these coastal Southern communities rely on blue-collar workers (Ocejo, 2017).

The fishing industry

Although most of the fishing families in this sample have been engaged in the industry for decades, either on their own or as a continuation of a multigenerational family business, the question of what comes next poses serious problems for the future of the fishing industry along the southern coast. Rising fuel costs, decreasing market prices, and increasingly strict environmental laws, not to mention the recurring threat of hurricanes and lasting damage of the Deepwater Horizon oil spill, are forcing many fishing families out of the business. Of these many interrelated problems, fuel prices were among the challenges most frequently mentioned by the fishermen and women. Many remember when fuel was cheaper and shrimp prices were higher, making it easier to earn a profit off a day's work. Neal, who has been in the fishing business in South Carolina for almost 40 years, explains how difficult it is to make a profit from shrimping today: "Well, average, you try to at least get 1,000 pounds a day to try to—'cause I burn about 200 gallons of fuel a week, that's $620, so you try to get at least 1,000 pounds of shrimp, and that's about $2,000, then you got to pay your crew." However, he reflects on how the profit margins have changed throughout the years:

> Back in the old days you used could make money on five and all days when it was 17 cent, 30 cent a gallon fuel, but nowadays you got to try to set your sights a little higher. Like I just took my 55-foot nets off and put my 70-foot nets on to try to catch more.

Although the high fuel costs have negatively impacted many along the coasts, fuel prices notoriously rise and fall.

The evolving fuel cost to market prices dynamic caused more challenges in the industry, as it was slow to change: "When the fuel prices and everything went so high it was like $4 a gallon on fuel and a lot of people had to back out of [the industry]. Of course, since fuel and everything has gone down and it seems like the shrimping is coming back." Randy explains the impact of fuel prices on the local North Carolina shrimping community: "There's a bunch of people now looking for boats and everything because they've heard of all the money that was made, and now there's people thinking that it's that easy, but they may get fooled. They might want to get rid of their boat next summer." Randy highlights how quickly the industry can go from profitable to almost destitute with the changes in the season and fluctuating fuel prices.

Other fishermen, instead of mentioning rising costs, recount how profitable the industry has become in recent years compared with when they were fishing full time. Makeley describes the changes he has seen per pound of flounder:

> We come home and deal them to the fish dealer [for] $360, 12 cent a pound. That same catch of Flounder now is $11,000. ... I like to do it, but it didn't make no money. Spot is three cent, five cent. That's the reason I said I was born too soon. They're now about $1.50.

He has fished along the North Carolina coast for over 80 years, starting out with his father as a child, which influences how he views the prices fishermen can get for their catch now compared with those in the past.

While the price per pound of some fish has increased, other types of seafood, especially shrimp, have not seen the same increases and instead are faced with more competition and lower profit margins. The influx of imported shrimp has also created a major problem for the domestic fishing industry. Wayne has watched the Louisiana shrimp industry's cycles from the 1970s until today. Aside from fuel prices, the biggest factor he sees harming the local industry is imported shrimp:

> The boats were making some money, but then all of the sudden, I guess in the mid-80s, they started doing first these pond-raised shrimp that came out of South America. And then before you knew it, they had all these shrimp that was coming out of these Asian countries. In 2011 we are going to consume 85 percent imported shrimp in the United States.

Imported shrimp are sold at a lower price than domestically caught shrimp despite the unsustainable farming practices and the near slave labor conditions in international shrimp production as well as the superior taste of domestic shrimp (Burdeau, 2015; Nosowitz, 2015). The United States is the largest importer of shrimp in the world, with shrimp representing the number one seafood item in the country: Americans, on average, consumed 4.6 pounds of shrimp, and 16.1 pounds of seafood overall per person, in 2018 (Kerns, 2020). However, between 85% and 95% of the shrimp are imported, coming from Ecuador as well as China, Thailand, India, and Vietnam (Wood, 2020). In 2018, the US fishing industry as a whole brought in 9.4

billion pounds of seafood valued at $5.6 billion, with lobster, crabs, salmon, scallops, and shrimp being the most valuable products (Island Free Press, 2020).

Sammy, from Mississippi, places the responsibility for current problems in the shrimping industry on government policies that favored imported over domestic shrimp: "It's a dying industry and the government is the one that killed it. It wasn't just the Vietnamese people that came to this country. All this free trade with everybody and we got five countries that deliver seafood and they cut our throats." Although he has seen the problems that have arisen between Vietnamese and white fishermen (as will be discussed), he places the blame on the free trade agreements of the late 1980s that increased imports of shrimp as well as countless other products into the country at dramatically lower prices than their domestically produced counterparts, and that continue to be a site of tension between fishermen and government entities (Burdeau, 2015).

Although imported shrimp continue to have a negative impact on shrimp prices, there are organizations fighting back against the influx of foreign shrimp into US markets. Richard was one of the first people willing to buy shrimp from Vietnamese fishermen in Mississippi. He explains his work with the Southern Shrimp Alliance in response to the influx of imported shrimp: "We filed a trade action with the United States Department of Commerce ... and we won it. They started putting tariffs on these different countries. ... It was to inform people of the difference between our domestic shrimp and the pond-raised shrimp." The increasing emphasis on local food has made consumers more aware of where their food comes from, but with the exception of what is sold in coastal communities or in stores, such as Whole Foods, that label the origins of some of their seafood, it may be more difficult to find domestic seafood, even for a consumer who wants to avoid buying imported products.

Other fishing communities focus on the environment and changes within the local community itself that have little to do with fuel costs or government policies but continue to impact the fishing industry. The environmental changes occurring in and around the water are undeniable to people who have built their lives on the sea. Andrew has been around the water of South Carolina his entire life; he started fishing with his father over 70 years ago, and he has seen irreversible changes in the oceans:

> My daddy used to buy oysters from the black people, and the small ones, he'd take them and shovel them out in the

51

bottom of the creek and then he could go there and take them back up and get big old single oysters. Now that has disappeared. If you take them and throw them out there in the bottom of the creek and go back, they die. Our environment has changed, and God only knows why.

While Andrew acknowledges the changes he has seen in the water with little attention to the possible causes, other fishermen are quick to point out the cause of those environmental changes: "Pollution is a big deal now, because sometimes we'll have red tide in the [Chesapeake] Bay real bad, and I think that [is] affecting stuff a tremendous amount." Kevin recounts the first time he saw a red tide, a harmful algal bloom, ten or 12 years earlier: "It doesn't look good and some years it'll smell real bad when you're going through it. ... It was hard to find any good water. ... When it comes through, all the fish in the crab pots or crabs, it'll just kill everything." In regard to possible causes of the red tide, he continues: "Just runoff, and in the country for some reason everybody wants to go to every coast." The recent influx of people to the coast, as Kevin notes for Virginia, and the increasing coastal population's impact on climate change are not isolated to that segment of coastal communities. About 29 percent of the US population, or 94 million people, live along the Atlantic and Gulf coasts, with growth continuing every year from 2000 to 2016, except in 2005 and 2006, the years hurricanes Katrina, Rita, and Wilma decimated the coast (Cohen, 2018).

Fred describes the changes he has seen in North Carolina around the water: "I'd say the two biggest changes are there's more of a non-commercial presence on the water. There's more docks. There's more houses. There's more people riding around in boats. ... The other thing is there is at least a little bit less of everything that we've been trying to catch." He has been in the fishing industry for 25 years and has seen a gradual decrease in the availability of seafood in his local waters. The influx of more people to the coast causes significant problems for the sustainability of local waterways (Satterthwaite, 2009). Rocky, one of the youngest captains in the South Carolina region, who took over his father's business at age 15, lays out the three major factors he has seen decimate the fishing industry around Charleston:

> You got all these people here and they're building houses up and down the road. You're on deep water lots. People can put yachts here ... I saw the change in Charleston after Hugo in '89. ... The creek was slowing down but there was still a

lot of boats here. ... Then people started wanting to come here. Let's don't take out people's livelihoods unless they're ready to leave. There's a lot of people that wasn't ready to leave this that had to leave. ... And imported shrimp, and I don't really touch into much of that because it's not as big an issue as it used to be. Our issue now is we don't have no new guys. We don't have younger people wanting to do this and the older guys don't really want to teach younger guys to do it no more. They're not even building new boats over here on this side no more.

The influx of people wanting to live along the coast, coupled with an older and more diverse population compared to the rest of the country, leads to dense population clusters around the coastal US (Cohen, 2018). These new migrants to the coast are not seeking to make a living on the water, and the industry is aging, making the future uncertain. Kevin describes the aging population in his local Virginia crabbing community: "I don't think it will be nobody crabbing because the average crabber in Virginia is 62 years old now. There's nobody young. I'm the youngest person, at 46, that's doing it." Up and down the coasts, age is a major factor in the future of commercial fishing.

Living along the water means dealing with the inevitable hurricanes. The East Coast industry vividly remembers Hurricane Hugo in September 1989, while the Gulf Coast is still dealing with the aftermath of Hurricane Katrina in 2005 and the subsequent Deepwater Horizon oil spill in 2010. Although the demand for local seafood is present along the coast, it is vulnerable to changes in nature as well as the effects of human-created disasters. Donna discusses her Louisiana restaurant's seafood gumbo:

Well, before the oil spill we put oysters in it, and then once the oil spill came the oysters went up to so much money that we had to cut—it was like $60 a gallon of oysters. ... It's still great without the oysters, now we have shrimp, crabmeat, sausage, and ham.

Although the gumbo is still delicious without the oysters, the oil spill has caused other problems that are not as easily remedied: "We went from doing like 150 people on the weekends to like 40 and 50 people. ... The fishermen was our business." Her restaurant relies on recreational fishermen for a majority of its clientele, but the oil spill, which occurred shortly before Memorial Day in 2010, obliterated tourism that summer.

Almost every fishing family has at least one hurricane story. Joanie describes her experience, when she was 18 years old, during Hurricane Hugo on her and her husband's shrimp boat:

> We ended up the Cooper River and went way up in a creek, and you did a lot of praying; it was scary, and people down the river from us, their boats turned over, sank, and people died just from trying to save their boats. ... It was no fear, we had no children at the time, and it was—you wanted to protect your livelihood.

Joanie and her husband, as well as many other local shrimpers, had to make the decision to try to protect their boat, and subsequently their main source of income, or to seek safety from the category four hurricane that ended up killing 27 people in South Carolina alone and causing billions of dollars in damage along the Atlantic seaboard.

Others work to ensure the safety of seafood consumed after disasters. Pete explains his role in testing the water quality throughout the New Orleans area after Katrina: "We sampled from the third week after the storm and sampled all of Lake Pontchartrain 'cause that's where everything pumped into, and the whole east side of Lake Borgne, and everything so far has looked good—no contamination." His wife, Clara, continues: "I've eaten some of the shrimp, I just couldn't wait. I told my friend, I said 'I'm having withdrawals. I have to have shrimp.' So she caught some and gave me some and we fried and boiled some. It was real good." Although the water is safe and they have resumed eating local seafood when they are able, their fishing business was still stalled because the infrastructure necessary to process and refrigerate the product was destroyed by Katrina. Pete sums it up succinctly: "We don't have any more infrastructure. ... It will cost two and three quarters to three million just to get started again. ... We have no fuel. We have no ice. We have no water." Until the docks were rebuilt there was no way to sell the product, and at this point their only hope was one working dock. Until the military brought generators or someone else stepped in, the lack of water, fuel, and ice made it impossible to operate on a normal scale.

The oil spill has also negatively impacted the fishing industry of the Gulf Coast particularly. Though hurricanes cause property damage and are life threatening for those in their path, the oil spill posed a new problem: the use of harmful chemicals, or the dispersant, combined with the oil itself, and the government's decision to flush fresh water into the fragile ecosystem, which killed off the local fish and oyster populations. Mark explains the problems he has sourcing oysters since the oil spill:

> He had the best around but since the BP oil spill, it pretty much wiped him out in that part of Grand Isle. It wasn't so much the oil spill; it was more of the Davis Pond. When they opened Davis Pond to try and flush some of the oil out of the marsh, it was the freshwater that killed a lot of his oysters. I haven't seen him selling oysters since the BP oil spill.

Although Mark works in the offshore oil industry in Louisiana, his problem sourcing seafood for his clients reflects how interconnected the oil and fishing industries are in the Gulf of Mexico. He continues: "When our oil industry is bad everything is bad over here. That's just the way we work. Everything surrounds the oil industry." Although the relationship between fishermen and the oil industry seems counterintuitive, the oil industry is a major employer in communities along the coast, providing commercial fishermen with customers for their product.

Oysters are not the only shellfish impacted by the oil spill; crabs also showed signs of being impacted. Al, a bait shop owner in Louisiana, has seen reproductive problems in the crab population since the oil spill, which he attributes to the dispersant:

> A dispersant was something to sink the oil, dissipate the oil, get rid of it by some means. Roundup is a weed killer. You spray it to get rid of the grass by some means. Any chemical, or every chemical has a label on it that says it's harmful in some kind of way by some means. So I guess too much of it could hurt. I guess too much oil could do the same thing. ... I think we just have to wait and see what takes place next year.

Although the fishing industry's rebound has been slow following the oil spill, there have been environmental downturns before, and in most cases, it just takes time for the fish to come back. However, unlike in previous years when the oil spills were much smaller or when changes in the environment eventually worked themselves out with little to no human intervention, the effects of the Deepwater Horizon oil spill may not go away as quickly.

The government reaction to the oil spill also bred distrust between the fishing industry and government decision-makers. Donald elaborates on the impact of the oil spill in Mississippi:

> The dispersant, from what we're hearing, is outlawed overseas. You know, they can't use it in Europe and all. But they can use it over here. ... We can put it in our waters. That's the only scary part of the oil industry now. If it makes our products to where they're not going to reproduce or if it's going to be a long-term effect. But if next season gets back to normal, that's what nobody really knows. Not even the biologist, much less people.

Although it has been a decade since the BP oil spill, the lingering effects can still be seen, especially in large marine life that have longer life spans including dolphins and turtles, as well as in deepwater zones and wetlands. While the oil is gone, the areas surrounding the blowout of the oil rig are still contaminated and biodiversity continues to be reduced in those areas. Although protections were put in place after the oil spill, subsequent administrations negated all those protections and opened up all coastal waters to offshore drilling while reducing oversight, making a future disaster not only possible, but probable (Ma, 2019).

Hurricanes and oil spills are not the only dangers faced by those who make a living off the ocean. The boat itself can be treacherous. Rocky describes some of the more difficult things he has seen in his 30 years on the water off the coast of South Carolina:

> People call me a hard captain because I make people realize you've got to stay out of the ropes 'cause I seen that guy die. It took him all the way up the block up there and he hung there and it actually hung him. ... I've seen boats burn. I've went up and got people off of boats burning. Fire is a scary thing on a boat 'cause you don't have much time.

The risk of severe bodily harm and death are daily realities that fishermen have to navigate to safely bring their catch to shore each day.

Despite the continual changes among the fishing communities, there is a deep-seated distrust of the government and environmental agencies, which are seen as having questionable or misguided motives. Government interference was frequently mentioned as a source of frustration within the industry. The most frequently mentioned aspect of this frustration was the turtle excluder: "The turtle excluder is a device which excludes turtles, and the endangered species was the Kemp's Ridley turtle. But I looked in the encyclopedia; they're not even indigenous to the Gulf of Mexico. ... I have never caught one in my life." Leroy explains that even though he has been a shrimper for 30 years, he has never caught one of the endangered turtles, yet he still has to comply with the federal laws. He continues: "This turtle excluder is not only a device inside that net; it's a 32-inch hole right in front of your bag where all the shrimp go and you lose about a third of your profit. ... There's very few business that can actually operate with a third loss." Although he tried to hold on to the business, he ended up closing it and joining his sister's bakery instead.

David sums up most of the fishing industry's stance:

> It's the hardest thing you can do because you are competing with the weather, you're competing with everything, everything is against you. Every time you leave the dock you are in the hole. It's hard to get in that mindset that every time you leave the dock you have to make a certain amount of money.

David has been working with his family on boats off the coast of South Carolina for over 40 years, and similar to those who focused on the changes in fuel and shrimp prices, he has seen the challenges of life in the fishing industry yet has no intention of closing his business. Despite the numerous obstacles faced by those trying to make a living from the sea, most, including David, would not change anything about their lifestyle. Julie explains how the overall scenery and nature surrounding the South Carolina waterways is a continuous source of inspiration for her to continue in the industry:

> I think being out on the water, not dealing with the people—you deal with the weather and the bugs. You've got your beautiful sunrises, the sunsets, and there's eagles and ospreys. The scenery out there is—to me it's worth it. I love the water. I love everything to do with fishing. I love the beaches, the lighthouse, just everything out there is so relaxing, even if you're dead tired.

For others it is not as much about the scenery as it is the fresh seafood. Makeley explains that, despite the trials and tribulation of being a commercial fisherman in North Carolina, he loved the experience and relied on the sea for most of his food: "That's the way it was, but I kept right on doing it 'cause I loved to fish and loved to shrimp and loved to do it. I loved to eat them. I had what I wanted to eat, see, when I was commercial fishing. I had shrimp, flounder, scallops—whatever I wanted." For some, the water represents freedom. Danny explains that he kept fishing throughout his 30-plus-year career as a commercial crabber in South Carolina because of his overall love of the water: "It's kind of rewarding and I just like the freedom."

The ocean's products, freedom, and natural surroundings continue to keep people tied to a struggling industry; yet in almost every case, even though they see the problems surrounding them, the people involved are not willing to seek another form of employment and continue to hope the industry will improve. As with any industry that has to rely on nature for its profit margins, the fishing industry in the Southeast is vulnerable to environmental changes, hurricanes, as well as government policies that flood the market with imported products at lower cost and fuel prices that fluctuate almost daily. Similar to other producers, the passion for their craft and the intrinsic value of their labor sustains the industry and its workers as they continue to ride the waves of change with the hope of continuing to be a vital part of the local community food scene (Ocejo, 2017; Borer, 2019).

The fishing community

The relationship between the water and the seasons is integral to life near the water. Jan reflects on growing up on a North Carolina barrier island, with the mainland only accessible by boat: "Most of the food on the coast is seasonal, and depending on the year—in the early 1900s there were boats that travelled from wherever you were living at to bring you the staples like sugar, salt, flour, coffee." Communities that were not connected to the mainland had to rely on boats for supplies, but this isolation also bred a sense of self-sufficiency as people made do with what was available. Jan goes on to describe the hardships that came with the changing seasons: "The wintertime might have been the hardest; they would, in the fall of the year, they would catch a lot of fish that could be split and salted in the barrels. And they were used to supplement the food." Although sourcing food was essential, Jan elaborates that it only represents one aspect of relying on the sea for life:

> They made fireplaces out of shells ... they break the shells apart and get them as fine as they can and then mix lime with them and make it into like a cement. And then they

take the larger shells and glue them together with the lime
and somehow come up with a fireplace.

Making fireplaces from shells that have washed up on the beach was
only one example. The houses along the beach had also been built
or repaired with wood that washed up on the beach after storms and
even from ships that had been wrecked along the coast. Every aspect
of daily life was intertwined with the ocean.

Life on the water also meant seafood was a major component in the
diets of people near the water. Julie explains how growing up on the
water of South Carolina impacted her family's diet: "I've always eaten
plenty of seafood, and usually between the deer and seafood you keep
your freezers pretty full around here, so you don't have to buy a whole
lot of meat." Although this statement calls to mind the middle- and
upper-class ability to rely only on locally sourced food, Julie's comments
reflect another approach to food culture that is not solely associated
with local food movements or healthier lifestyles. Simply put, it is the
way of life in coastal communities that historically reflected the seasonal
availability of what could be sourced from the water and the dearth of
grocery stores or other readily available food supplies.

The isolation created by life on the water also fostered a sense of
community among those who shared that lifestyle. As Mila explains,
growing up on a small island off the coast of North Carolina, where
her family has always lived, instilled in her an understanding of the
need to work hard to survive. However, despite the hardships, the
importance of community solidarity was as necessary as hard work to
combat the isolation of island life:

> We're just hard-working people. When you grow up and
> you're around the water, people have always had to work
> for what they got. Great-grandparents, when they went
> clamming or whatever, they sold those to pay a bill. And
> to eat of course, but if they didn't get it handed to them.
> ... Island people, they worked hard for what they got. It's
> just a community, a close-knit community. And we help
> each other.

This sense of community extends throughout the coastal South.
Frank explains that although the commercial fishing industry is very
competitive, the local Mississippi community is also supportive: "When
it comes down to helping somebody, I really believe it don't matter
who you are. You're going to get help and that's just something—that's

where the brotherhood of the whole commercial fishing industry." Although people can rely on the community for help, this can also lead to problems. Jamie explains that competition among crabbers at times leads to theft or vandalism: "Well, all us crabbers battle with each other. ... Like say he knows I'm catching a lot of crabs and he ain't, he might come to my area and steal some of my traps and take them somewhere else, and you know, it's a dirty game." However, such vandalism is rarely mentioned in the oral histories; instead, the resounding emphasis is on how strong the community solidarity was during difficult times.

Despite the problems caused by competition, the shared experiences around the water have also facilitated the development of a sense of community grounded in the immigrant history of the area. Corky, a retired fisherman raised along the Mississippi coast, describes the variety of languages and cultures he was surrounded by in the community as a child: "At home we all spoke Slavish. I guess the French people the same way, most of them came from Louisiana; the Polish from Pollock. Well, they all came down here to the seafood industry—fish and shrimp and oysters, and we all got along pretty good." Corky's parents migrated to the Mississippi coast from Bobovisco a coastal town in Croatia by way of Ellis Island, and together with other immigrants in the community they worked in the fishing industry and founded a lodge in the community where everyone could gather. The lodge continues to be a community gathering point decades later.

The sense of community extends beyond helping each other to include local business transactions. Joanie explains how her South Carolina seafood market barters with the local fisherman and others in the community for work around the dock: "They do a lot of bartering, trading seafood for services, and it's a good way to—it's just like the old days what people used to do, trade their vegetables, trade their fish. I mean we still do that, that's still active." Her twin sister, Ellie, continues: "There's a big group of folks that just love to scratch each other's backs. They're not in it for the money. This is not a money-making business. You're here for the love of what you do and the people that work around you." The love of the community and of the water is integral to the continuation of the local fishing community. The solidarity created within fishing communities provides a necessary resource to an industry and its related businesses that are highly vulnerable to nature's unpredictability, and this translates to depending on one another.

Although the local community is an essential factor in the survival of commercial fishing, not everyone in these areas is happy with the industry's dominant presence. Susan, who runs a restaurant in a coastal Virginia community, explains that although some new transplants are annoyed by the noise of the commercial fishing boats, she has a deep appreciation for the work they represent: "They work hard. They provide us with some really wonderful seafood. If it wasn't for the watermen on the Northern Neck, we'd be in trouble. ... I appreciate the watermen. They work hard, they provide us with a good product. And I think we should support them." As the demographics of coastal communities change, the noise produced by commercial fishing is seen as a problem instead of as evidence of thriving local businesses in the way restaurants and stores symbolize an economically successful downtown district.

Along the coast there is a direct relationship between the fishing industry and the local restaurants, with many restaurants selling locally caught seafood. Although the idea of serving local products at restaurants has become increasingly popular throughout the US, it is still a struggle for restaurants to maintain a steady profit margin, and many have closed despite the national attention on local food (Biery, 2018). Joanie and Ellie's market connects chefs to local shrimpers, among others in the industry. Joanie describes the changes she is seeing in how the local business scene resonates with consumers who are seeking local food: "I think, just think back to supporting your local businesses. You know, there are tons of families out there that are starting, you know, young people starting, farmers." Her sister jumps in and continues: "I see that's making a little bit more of a comeback than the fishing industry with the younger people...not everyone is set to, you know, go to college. ... Give the people a chance that are willing to work hard and buy from those local businesses." Her sister, Ellie, builds on these comments to emphasize how important the process that brings fresh seafood to their store is for consumers to understand: "[Fishermen] come back, and then our unloading process, and then it gets to the counter; but you know, it's not shipped across waters for weeks. It is here for everyone to enjoy and it's a healthy option." The importance of the superiority of local seafood resonates with chefs and consumers willing to spend a little more money on a better product (Nosowitz, 2015).

Restaurants, with the exception of the most popular ones, need a reliable consumer base within the local community to stay open, because tourism can only sustain a restaurant for part of the year. Mila explains how the tight-knit local community has come to see her coastal North Carolina restaurant, which has been in operation for 30 years, as a gathering place: "We're the only locally owned restaurant on the island now. There are several others but we're the only one that are the locals, and [islanders] love to come up here and drink their coffee and tell tales about who caught something bigger." Emma began working as a cook for Mila after she stopped fishing commercially. She describes the unfortunate changes that have occurred among island restaurants over the years: "They're all gone. They had four or five on here and they're all gone ... really the fish houses are gone, and the restaurants are gone." The fish houses supplied local restaurants with fresh seafood, but as pollution and federal regulations increasingly impacted the fishing industry, the packing houses and later the restaurants began to disappear. Now, only one locally owned restaurant serving locally caught seafood remains on the island.

Sourcing seafood, similar to all fresh products, is dependent on seasonal variation. Richard, the chef at a well-established seafood restaurant in a major tourist area near the Virginia coast, explains that blue crabs cannot be caught in the winter when the water is ice cold, any more than an heirloom tomato can be harvested in the spring: "We were a regional seafood restaurant, and that region has gotten bigger every year, it seems like. It's not just regional Chesapeake Bay, Virginia, North Carolina, anymore; it has to expand." The demand for seafood and the expectation of a set menu has forced the restaurant to deviate from being a regional seafood restaurant. He continues:

> In the middle of January, when someone comes in and says, "Is your lump crabmeat from Virginia?"—obviously not, because it's 12 degrees outside and nobody's crabbing and the crabs aren't even crabbing. They're underneath the sand. ... But you got to be 12 months out of the year, so you have to stay as loyal to the region as you can within reason.

Richard works to source seafood from local fishermen, but "local" has to take on a loose definition to meet consumer demand regardless of the seasonal reality.

Despite the historical role of local seafood in coastal communities, the plethora of restaurants seen today selling local products is relatively recent. Yet the commercial fishermen and women providing them with local seafood were there long before the resurgence of local and seasonal restaurants. Today, Charleston is known for being at the forefront of the local food movement, featuring dozens of restaurants serving locally sourced food including seafood. However, despite this culinary renaissance, it was not always the case in the city's restaurants.

Kimberly and her husband sold fresh shrimp in the city during the early 1990s: "At the time he was selling like 400 pounds of shrimp to RB's Restaurant and all these other restaurants in Charleston were using imported shrimp. ... The best thing I did was put the seafood in the back of the truck and go downtown." She would show up at a restaurant with a variety of seafood including shrimp, stone crab claws, mahi, and tuna, among others, and show them to the chefs. This became the foundation of her family's seafood business, which lasted 20 years until she retired, and local seafood is a hallmark of the Charleston restaurant scene today.

As consumers increasingly support the local food movement, the demand for local seafood is growing, but the increased demand goes beyond a desire for local food. William explains why his Virginia restaurant focuses on local products: "I think it's more than local food. They want a local flavor, and why wouldn't you? If you're coming to an area, the last thing I'm gonna want is a chain restaurant. You want flavors from that area, beers, wine from that area, foods from that area." Local food is a way to engage with a place in the same way that wine is a reflection of the terroir, to be consumed either while looking out the window onto the land where the vines are grown, or miles away to recall the place and time where the wine was made. Local products allow customers to believe they are consuming a place and having an authentic experience in a way that mass-produced products do not (Peterson, 1997; Johnston and Baumann, 2010).

Seafood serves a similar purpose as wine for the ability to taste the place where it was grown. For example, oysters reflect the distinct qualities of the water where they were harvested, making place an integral component in taste variations. Georgio explains that when he immigrated from Croatia, he had never seen or tasted a shrimp. Today, he refuses to source anything but local shrimp for his restaurant:

> Our seafood, which is very important, it's a good fresh local seafood. ... We don't use any foreign seafood products. ... The Gulf of Mexico produces one of the best seafoods in the world. ... It's just something about it: it's rich, it's healthy, and it's just simple, good, good quality seafood.

The superiority of local seafood is a driving factor for many restaurants, not only the prestigious restaurants of Charleston with their award-winning chefs and elite clientele. It is true as well for the small restaurants tucked in small towns across the South, which are often forgotten in discussions of local food, despite the fact that many of these restaurants pre-date the renowned restaurants central to the current local food movement.

William, the chef at a coastal Virginia restaurant, highlights the uniqueness of the region's blue crab: "The flavor of the blue crab, the Chesapeake Bay blue crab, is so delicate, so beautiful. We use an old Tangier recipe, and it's got simple ingredients. ... It's pretty simple but in that simplicity is just incredible beauty." He goes on to explain what makes Tangier cuisine and culture so unique:

> One of the things that has kind of haunted me or been with throughout my life is kind of the dilution of culture. I think one of the things that's always stuck with me is the culture of Tangier. ... You realize, wow, that little island was preserved for so long. All of its micro-culture was preserved for so long because of its isolation.

The simplicity and geographical specificity of the crab cake recipe that can be traced to the history of a small island off the Virginia coast allows consumers to connect with the place and with generations of people who would have made their living and sought sustenance from the ocean (Johnston and Baumann, 2010). Although for many tourists this represents a foreign way of life, the attempt to recreate the past through a dish allows consumers a small taste of what that life may have been like, and it gives credence to the demand for local or craft products that were forgotten in all but the small communities whose livelihoods depended on these traditional practices.

As tourists continue to seek out local products, the focus is often placed on the restaurant, not the local markets, yet these retail markets sustain the local fishing industry. Frank explains how he has been able to keep his family's Mississippi-based shrimping business open by maintaining a local retail market despite the rising cost of fuel and decreasing cost of shrimp resulting from an influx of imported shrimp from overseas markets: "We sell our shrimp to locals. ... If you can come and market your shrimp right off the boat to the public, or to different outlets that you can get lined up, you can get an average $4 for our shrimp instead of $1.50." He notes that this is not the first time his family has struggled: "It was very bad in the early 80s and several of my family members lost their boats and homes. We've seen bad times but as long as there is demand for fresh shrimp, I'm going to try to hang in there as long as I can." Financial struggles are not a new phenomenon for most of those in the commercial fishing industry, and even though fuel prices have risen, the consumer demand for local shrimp provides a degree of stability for shrimpers who rely on the retail market.

The desire for locally sourced food extends far beyond the demand for local produce or meats. In coastal communities the demand for local seafood is paramount for both customers and purveyors, not just for restaurants. Eddie explains how his local North Carolina community relies on seafood markets to connect the fishermen to the customer: "I want people to have good food and I want them to have quality food and I'm proud of the quality of my seafood. And people pay for quality. They pay for it [in] other places and they'll pay for it here." His market is a source of pride because he is able to sell local seafood caught by fishermen in his community directly to consumers for their tables at home. He is also the main source of seafood for the restaurants in the area that choose to highlight local products. Mila explains that she sources from Eddie for her restaurant: "We buy from Eddie, and we buy from a couple local fisherman that has the blue fish or whatever, and we get our meat from Billy [the local butcher]." The connections between fishermen, markets, and restaurants is not uncommon in the craft food scene, and this extends to people being able to take local products home with them more frequently. As sociologist Michael Borer (2019) describes in his research on craft beer in Las Vegas, it is the strength of these connections across industry players that helps these businesses survive and thrive, especially in areas that may not initially fully support the endeavor.

This sense of pride in a product is common among members of the craft food movement and it can be seen in the local fishing community as well, with one caveat: the price local products demand is difficult to justify for producers who have grown up around the industry. Ellie explains the difficulty in maintaining a high standard of quality and sourcing at her South Carolina market without demanding the exorbitant prices that are commonly asked for those products: "We try our very best to keep everything local, fresh, something we would eat. And it's hard, but the worst thing going on right now is the prices we're having to charge. I am almost embarrassed daily to have to serve a customer and especially regular customers." She elaborates on the shift of seafood from an everyday staple to a luxury: "It is a special day for anybody that I think could come in and buy dinner for their family at a fresh seafood market without being some trash from another country." The financial difficulties prompted Ellie and her family to expand the business from only selling fresh seafood to include a small restaurant: "We started 'cause things were getting really, really hard. We did not know if we were going to make it, so we thought, what can we do to subsidize—you know, to help a little bit? So we started with a fryer on the dock cooking." This simple business has morphed into a small catering company that does family events including weddings.

Richard, the chef at a locally owned Virginia seafood restaurant, explains that it is difficult to source enough of a product because of competition from other states, especially New York:

> A lot of the seafood that they—if it's not coastal above them, from Canada, it's bought down here, which is always still a battle, because everything else is softshell season right now. And the New York people will pay serious high dollars for softshell crabs, when we've got to try to stop the trucks from going up there, to give us our share. But we won't pay as much because we can't charge what they charge.

He describes how the restaurant has dealt with these sourcing problems: "You find smaller farmers who maybe don't have those connections with New York, with the Washington, DC, markets, and they're just doing it for a short season. ... I think the biggest thing is just to develop relationships with them." The high demand from urban areas makes it difficult to keep local seafood in local restaurants. Urban restaurants paying higher prices than the local market can sustain creates tension, and it is up to chefs to develop relationships with small fishing businesses to ensure a portion of the softshell crabs, in this particular case, stay in the restaurants near the water where they were harvested.

The relationship between chefs, customers, and fishermen is exemplified by recent efforts to promote "trash" or "under-loved" fish in restaurants. While climate change and unsustainable fishing practices have altered what seafood can be pulled from local waters, there are still plenty of fish available, but they are typically lesser-known and therefore less expensive fish such as dogfish, selling for 20 cents per pound on the East Coast. A group of local fishermen, responding to demand for local fish, partnered with local chefs to raise consumer awareness regarding these lesser-known types of fish. While some of these programs provide the fish to chefs for free until the demand takes off, others focus on marketing endeavors to raise consumer awareness with the goal of making under-loved fish present in grocery stores as well as restaurants, thus furthering the financial solvency of the local fishing industry. Although seemingly a new endeavor, there is a history of success in making under-loved fish financially successful by partnering with chefs and consumers; for example, a once under-loved fish, hake, became so popular that the fishermen could not keep up with the increased demand (Wilcox, 2017). Another example is the nationwide Chefs Collaborative organization that works to connect chefs to local, sustainable producers, whose Seafood Solutions program hosts "Trash Fish" dinners across the country (Chefs Collaborative, ND). These types of partnerships offer two examples of how chefs, consumers, and the local fishing industry have worked together to establish relationships and raise awareness around local seafood.

Gender and race in commercial fishing

Historically commercial fishing was mainly done by men, but women continue to be a presence in the fishing industry through their roles in packing houses and in accompanying their fathers or husbands on their boats. Emma explains that as a child she was responsible for helping her father, a commercial fisherman in North Carolina, because at the time there were no boys in her family and her older sisters had jobs at a local factory:

> I was with my Daddy because he said every time he went down to get in the boat I was sitting there waiting for him, even when I was a little toddler. ... I was the one that always helped him because we didn't have the boys then. ... I'd take that boat and I'd go to that fish house and I'd sell those flounders for him so he could sleep. ... I loved the water the most.

Although this story reflects how she first started fishing, she continued in the industry as an adult, becoming a commercial fisherwoman herself. She explains: "You'd be down there in the scallop house opening scallops. We had a scallop house right down by the boat house. We'd catch the scallops. The men would catch them. I would catch them. Now, most of the women didn't go catch scallops like I did." A neighbor who worked in the scallop house would cook lunch for them while they helped fill her container of scallops, so she would not lose any money due to her loss of productivity while she took time out to prepare lunch for everyone. The sense of camaraderie within these fishing communities runs deep across generations of families that have long worked from the same docks.

Susan started crabbing on her own at age 13. She recounts a story from her earliest days on the water off the coast of Virginia:

> [Other crabbers] were so amazed that a girl would be doing this, and especially my mother's daughter; she would never have done this, but I like it. And they loved my grandfather. ... I saw one of the crab men—a crabber, he was at my crab pot, and I thought oh my goodness he is taking my crabs. ... I went over there and pulled up my crab pot and it was just crammed pack full. ... Years later I found out he was putting crabs in my crab pot, because they thought it was wonderful that I was crabbing.

The fishing industry is often a family endeavor, with children learning from their parents and slowly becoming independent with their own small businesses and boats. Women were often integral to these efforts, even at an early age, despite the fishing industry being skewed heavily toward men as the main workers. Many of the women who work in the commercial fishing industry work in the packing houses. Emma explains how gender played a part in the North Carolina sector of the industry: "Some of the women, they mostly done the scallop houses. Now, I know one or two would go with their husbands. ... [My husband] worked on trawlers for a while. When he was on them big trawlers, I didn't go with them." As noted here, few women ran their own boats, and they mostly worked alongside their husbands on smaller commercial operations.

Julie, from South Carolina, describes some of the gendered dynamics she grew up with while helping her stepfather collect oysters:

> Tonging oysters is something I can do for about 15 minutes. It's definitely a man's job. I mean, it's all upper body strength. I always was the one that relieved or culled out all the stud he brought in in the tongs, so that's what I did as a child whenever I went out oystering.

Although she grew up around the water, she left the profession for several years to go into business with her now ex-husband. She explains her decision to leave the deer processing business she built with her ex-husband and return to commercial fishing:

> So I gave it up, the whole business, house and everything, and I went back to work on the water, being a single mother

to make the money that I needed to be able to raise my children. ... I had to stay on the water cause I can make good money at it.

Gender is a factor in the work and representation women experience in the commercial fishing industry, but interestingly those who choose to make a living on the water did not express any concerns with gender stereotypes or perceptions of their inability to work alongside men in the commercial fishing industry.

Race and immigration came up repeatedly in the conversations with members of the fishing community. These topics were particularly notable among the fishing communities along the Gulf Coast, which became home to a large portion of Vietnamese refugees following the Vietnam War, many of whom entered the fishing industry. Immigration has played a major role in fishing communities, with different groups coming to the coast at various points in time (Levin et al, 2010). Although some waves of immigration are only vague memories today, others are still seen as a problem. Andrew recalls that the Portuguese were some of the earliest commercial shrimpers in the Charleston area:

My cousins were not the first to start shrimping in Charleston. It was the Portuguese, my daddy and brother told me. ... There was a lot of Portuguese here in Charleston but I don't know what happened to them. ... We had one old Portuguese [man] down at the dock where I was. ... He's the only one left I ever seen.

Andrew explains that although his family was on the cutting edge of bringing diesel engines to the local fishing community in the early 1900s, they were not the ones who propelled the fishing industry in the area, which is attributed to Portuguese settlers. However, by the time Andrew started working alongside his father at the docks in the 1940s, most of the Portuguese had disappeared from the fishing industry.

William, a 70-year-old fisherman from South Carolina, recalls the race relations he was aware of growing up around the docks:

I think back on race relations, there were a lot more blacks in the seafood industry when I was younger. I mean many more. I don't think it was exactly intentional but the blacks usually picked shucking oysters and the whites, when they went out and did oysters, picked single oysters. ... They were making enough money to own their own boats, but there was almost this feeling that if they owned their own boat that the dock owners would discriminate against them and keep them from making money. By the mid–1980s there were some black boat owners.

In many cases along the East Coast, the role of race and immigration is only discussed in memories of the distant past, and no current examples were brought up in the oral histories regarding race relations in the region.

The Gulf Coast has a more recent memory of immigration and the changes it brought to the local fishing community. Frank discusses the connection between immigration and the local Mississippi-based fishing community. He begins by explaining that the early immigrants were from Eastern Europe, and today those last names are represented by doctors, lawyers, and businessmen in the local community:

> The last immigrants that come here, which was Vietnamese, they worked really hard. They sent the majority of their kids to school. ... Now you see that group of immigrants, a lot of the Vietnamese in this community, they all are business owners, doctors, lawyers. When people came here to work, they just wanted to better their kids. It's just a big cycle and it keeps repeating itself and that's one thing about the fishing business here. It was always for people with no education, people that couldn't speak the English language very well, they could get in the fishing business. ... How much money they made [was] determined by how hard they work. That's the same way I feel about my kids; if they want to go to college, hey, I'm going to support them 100 percent, but if they want to stay in the fishing business, then let's do it.

For many, the link between immigration and fishing is a reflection of hard work and the desire to create a better life for one's children. This feeling is shared among the members of the fishing community, with the emphasis being placed on the success of the next generation and the importance of valuing hard work as a means to achieve success.

Robert runs a Louisiana company that dries shrimp. He describes the evolution of drying shrimp in the region: "There was 21 dried shrimp platforms over the marsh, all Chinese-owned. When I really got into the business, I could remember about 12 different drying plants that were around. And now I could think of maybe four that's still existing." Robert's grandfather arguably had the first American-owned shrimp drying platforms in the marsh. He had become friends with some of the local Chinese shrimp driers, and over time they taught him the process of drying shrimp. Today, his business and those of the Chinese family who taught him remain open.

Although immigration along the Gulf Coast created collaboration opportunities for new industries to develop, not everyone looks back on those periods of history fondly. Many remember the privileges given to the Vietnamese because of their refugee status at the time. However, their discontent is not simply about the people; as with the Deepwater Horizon oil spill, it is about the impact of government interference on the fishing community, as Leroy explains:

> The only thing I disliked about it is that the Vietnamese got a lot of breaks that the American fisherman didn't get. They got low interest loans where the American fisherman couldn't apply for them. ... I think it's the United States government that was wrong—what they did, because they didn't give everybody the same opportunity. I have nothing against Vietnamese people; they're good, hardworking people.

Echoing studies about people's views on racial inequalities, whites support equality in principle but do not support government efforts to remedy racial and ethnic inequalities in society because they are viewed as "unfair handouts" or "pushing the issue" despite the long history of white advantages in the US economy (Bobo and Tuan, 2006; Omi and Winant, 2015; Bonilla-Silva, 2017).

For others, immigration is not a memory but is foundational to their families' experiences. Kimberly tells the story of her now deceased husband fleeing Cuba after Fidel Castro took over: "He was 14 years old when he came to this country. He picked eggplant and cucumbers in the fields down there and he learned English by watching Sesame Street on TV. ... Then his brother from Cuba came up and they were the first Cuban fishermen out of Shem Creek." Although he lived in the US for decades, he ran into problems with immigration services in 1998: "He was taken away in 1998, indefinite detention, and he was going to be deported back to Cuba, so for nine months I had to go back and forth to Atlanta to try to get him out, run our business every day." After nine months of imprisonment he was released: "Here we had gone from the pinnacle of our career. We were going to retire in another year, and he got out and I think we had less than $300 in the bank and maybe 20 pounds of shrimp. He got out and we started over from scratch." After re-establishing the business, he was diagnosed with cancer, and he passed away several years later, in 2006. After her husband's death, Kimberly was going to get out of the business but ended up being sponsored by the local restaurant industry to continue. Despite this support from the local industry, she shifted the focus exclusively to soft shell crabs:

> The Charleston restaurant community had a fundraiser for us because they wanted to help us keep the soft shell shedding part of the operation. ... They really wanted to hang on to us because we were one of the last vestiges of have it local, have a personal relationship with who you're buying your seafood from.

The relationship between Charleston chefs and local fishermen is a source of strength during difficult times, immigration and detainment being among them.

Such collaboration between the fishing industry and local establishments is not uncommon along the coasts. Eddie tells the story of Alberto, one of the men who works for him now, who he considers his best worker:

> Alberto as a young man swam the Rio Grande with a two-liter Pepsi bottle full of water. ... He made it to Texas and got on a shrimp boat and worked in the Gulf and then from there I think he wound up in Georgia on another shrimp boat and then he wound up here.

Although Alberto worked for one of Eddie's friends for nearly 13 years, one night the friend called Eddie, "and he said 'I'm going to give you Alberto. ... But you got to promise me he's got a job every day that he wants one.' I said, 'Well he's got one.'" After four years of working with Alberto, Eddie explains how they work together: "We've got to the point now we even think alike. When we work together, and we shrimp and when we shrimp, we split the money right down the middle." Though a touching story, underlying Eddie's comments are hints of how employment and racial inequality still impact immigrant workers' ability to find stable work even as where they work in the industry changes and they become employed by friends or colleagues of former employers (Royster, 2003).

Though long overlooked and often forgotten, Native Americans are still part of the local fishing scene and coastal communities, just as they were hundreds of years ago. Ashley, a member of the Virginia Pamunkey and an employee at the Pamunkey Indian Museum and Culture Center, explains how integral seafood is to traditional Pamunkey foodways. However, government laws and interventions have decimated those foodways by diverting funding from supporting fish hatcheries run by Indigenous groups along the coast and outlawing the catch of specific types of fish, such as shad, which is a staple in the Pamunkey diet:

> I hope that people understand how difficult it is for, not just indigenous communities, but small communities, small, rural communities who have traditions—especially when it comes to foodways—how hard it is to keep those traditions alive, and how there are people that really care and struggle to keep them alive. And we need help doing that.

For some people it is not about immigration or race in explicit discussions; it is about traditional foodways that were established generations ago that are being impacted by government interference, and these changes reflect a fraught history of genocide and displacement of Indigenous peoples.

Conclusion

Unlike the craft cocktail makers, elite butchers, and James Beard Award-winning chefs who are the focus of books, lifestyle media, and white middle- and upper-class self-identified foodies who seek out exclusive and authentic food experiences, the commercial fishermen and women across the southern coasts receive very little attention, even when their products are featured by award-winning chefs. While these now elite occupations are setting the standards for taste and are altering the food landscape across urban centers, as Richard Ocejo (2017) argues, they are no longer seen as the dirty, intensive-labor, and low-status jobs of the past. Today, they are legitimate employment options for the culturally savvy young adult. While this is true for the craft bartenders and butchers in New York City, the commercial fishing industry has not experienced the same revitalization in occupational status.

One explanation for this is that the labor of commercial fishermen and women is often invisible to the consumer. Not only does the work take place out of sight in the sea, marshes, and tidal creeks, this distance reduces what customers often seek from craft and local food movements and their products: a sensual experience, for example, of watching a craft cocktail be poured in a hidden speakeasy then instantly tasting the finished product. However, these fishermen and women do not live in the urban centers of the country. They call remote barrier islands and bayous home, removing their product a step further from the middle- and upper-class clientele who are likely to eventually purchase it. Yet the craft food movement is alive and well across the non-urban South, and fishermen, like farmers, are an essential though frequently invisible part of the success of the craft food movement.

Local Markets: Value-added Products at Farmers' Markets

As a child growing up in Virginia, when asked to describe our hometown, my classmates and I would say the cows outnumbered people almost three to one, and they still do today. The rolling hills leading up to the Blue Ridge Mountains on one side and the increasing sprawl of Washington, DC, on the other are dotted with cattle, red barns, and apple orchards, although today many of the orchards are gone and instead vineyards cover the hills. It is not uncommon to see a tractor on the main highway, and a majority of the full-time residents who do not make the hour-plus commute into northern Virginia are employed in some form of agricultural work. Homegrown food was not a rarity for my family. Both of my grandfathers planted large gardens as long as their health allowed and were frequently dropping off baskets of corn, tomatoes, and the always present zucchini at our back door. Despite growing up surrounded by agriculture, it was not until I was an adult and moved to the first of several college towns that I have called home in recent years that I was able experience a farmers' market for the first time.

It was here that I experienced produce that tasted better than anything I had bought in a store and saw the prices on the same types of canned goods that my grandmother had always kept lined on shelves in her pantry when I was a child. Over time, I frequented a farm stand where farmers were able to sell their produce, which was open every day of the week. Gradually I got to know the farmers and the staff of the farm stand, but it was not until the farm stand closed, from lack of consistent business, that people began to recognize how much they had relied on it. The farm stand was located in the middle of the city, and although the houses surrounding the store cost around a million dollars, just a couple blocks away property values plummeted and the violent crime rate skyrocketed. This area of the city was and continues to be one of the largest food deserts within the city limits, with nearly every grocery store having closed in the span of less than two years, which left only the farm stand as a source of fresh produce for the surrounding neighborhoods. Yet the stand still closed down because it was unable to cover the overhead costs and still pay the farmers. Four years later, the building still sits empty.

On the other side of the city, in a more youthful and affluent area, three farmers' markets thrive just blocks apart. Walking through one of the markets on a Saturday morning, I see many of the farmers I came to know at the farm stand as well as local chefs from the plethora of farm-to-table restaurants popping up across the city. A majority of the farms are run by young families, with husbands and wives or siblings working side by side. It's also not uncommon to see children helping their parents weigh produce or make change. On many Saturday mornings, especially in the mid- to late summer, when peppers and heirloom tomatoes fill the tables in a rainbow of colors, the market is so busy it is hard to get near the tables. However, while the city is home to half of the residents of color in the entire state, the farmers and market customers are a sea of white faces.

This chapter situates the experiences of farmers, especially women, who sell their goods at farmers' markets into the social and historical context of the region. Southern food culture is rife with gender inequality. The role of women, whether white or black, was traditionally relegated to labor within the home. This work included cooking at a time when processed food did not exist and before the introduction of modern technology such as electric stoves and refrigeration units. Everything was made from scratch and ensured that a family was sustained throughout the year. Despite the trend toward processed foods in the 1950s, rural areas across the South maintained a degree of traditional agriculture, cooking techniques, and canning practices. In most cases this was out of economic necessity, but it also shaped the development of Southern food culture, leaving lasting marks. Today, farmers' markets offer a space for the sale of these traditional value-added products, a product like jam or pickles where the producer has taken the raw ingredients and altered them in a way that adds value, as well as an alternative to industrial agriculture. This chapter addresses how the resurgence of a culture and subsequent spaces catering to slow and local foods makes it possible to revalue traditional food preparation techniques, specifically farming, canning, and baking from scratch, by placing them into the space of alternative productive relationships and valuing them as a form of knowledge and art existing in opposition to industrial, mass-produced food products.

The path to farming

The decision to call the South home and set up a farming enterprise is often a complex decision, but one many farmers heartily embrace. Celia, a white woman in her late thirties, explains why she decided to stay in Georgia even though it was different than where she grew up: "The South has just such a rich culture around food and rural life." She explains that even though there is a deep connection to rural life in the South, when she arrived ten years ago there were very few farms: "I felt like coming to the South was—I didn't go to the developing world, but the South was the farthest behind compared to the areas I had been in sustainable agriculture ... so in a way I could make more of an impact here." Hers was one of the earliest sustainable farms in the area, but today a small community of farmers focused on sustainable agriculture has been established in the area. The lack of a sustainable farming tradition in a region known for its agrarian past places the South behind other regions and also creates opportunities for small-scale farmers.

While some farmers maintain family traditions on the same land their family has owned for generations, others are returning to farming traditions from which they are generations removed. Charlotte's grandparents both had farms but left them to take up careers in Americus, Georgia, where her grandfather became a detective and her grandmother was able to take care of her and other people's children. When Charlotte, a white woman in her early forties, told her grandmother about her plan to start farming professionally, she was shocked someone would willingly choose such a hard life: "According to my grandmother it was much easier not being on the farm. In fact, when I told her what I planned on doing she was like, 'Why? You're well educated, why would you choose such a hard life?'" For many young farmers, the decision to farm was often met with resistance, at least initially, from friends and family. Jenny, a white woman in her early thirties, explains her family's hesitation when she and her husband decided to take over running her family's Georgia farm: "They were still not familiar with small diversified farms and did not think it was a good idea to farm for a living, especially since we both had college degrees, and they just saw it as a hard life and a hard way to make a living." Despite her parents' initial discouragement, they are happy the land is still being used and are now supportive of Jenny's decision to continue the tradition.

Other young farmers hoped to escape the family tradition of farming but could not resist the pull of the land. Jenni, a white women in her mid-twenties, explains that after college she moved to Atlanta and intended to live in the city, but over time she began to miss life on her family's farm:

> In Atlanta I felt like I was contributing to something I had
> no control over. And all these cool and exciting things were
> happening at home and I was so disconnected from it. ...
> I looked at my year away from the farm as more of a task
> than a blessing of being in Atlanta.

It took Jenni barely a year to return to the farm and the family business, where she has become an integral part of continuing the business and adapting the farm for the future.

Judith, a white woman in her late thirties, describes her trajectory to becoming a farmer: "I never expected to work in or around agriculture. When I met Joe, he was doing some food activism work that I thought was really intriguing and that is what opened the door to agriculture. Activism is definitely a part of what attracted us to agriculture." Although her grandfather was a sharecropper and has his own small farm, she had no intention of following in his footsteps until she met her husband, who was already involved in the food movement.

The ability to farm necessitates the availability of and access to land on which to grow crops. As evidenced by vineyard owners who have turned to wine to maintain their connection to the land, farmers across the South, and the United States as a whole, have a deep connection to the land, which they hope to preserve for future generations. A majority of the farmers in this sample are farming the land that their parents, grandparents, and great-grandparents farmed. In many cases the land was originally planted with tobacco, corn, and cotton. As time passed and prices fell, parts of the land were sold or switched over to other crops. Marjorie is an 81-year-old white woman who returned to farming years after her mother sold her land, when agricultural prices dropped after World War II. Despite the hardships associated with farming, her mother "thought the children needed to learn how to farm and make a living for their selves." She links farming to a collective family effort as well as survival. Land and knowledge are important aspects of farming. In many cases, both have been passed down for generations.

Making a profit is not the sole value of farming. Subsistence farming was an essential element of farmers' lives. Farming was done both for profit and for survival, providing a family with the necessary food to survive. Louise, a black woman who is a baker, was one of 15 children in her family. They sold tobacco and cotton, "but the food that we raised on the farm for the gardens, we did that for ourselves." The food grown during the summer would be canned or frozen, because "everything we had on the farm we had in the freezer to last us through the winter." Historically on farms across the South a majority of the land was used to grow cash crops such as tobacco and cotton, while a small portion was used for a kitchen garden that would provide the family with fresh vegetables during the summer and food to can or "put up" for winter when food became scarce (Engelhardt, 2011).

Many of the farmers in Mississippi come from families of farmers and farm on land that has been owned by their families for generations. Leann, a white woman who is a chicken farmer, watched her grandparents and parents farm the same land, which was purchased in the late 1920s. She "always wanted to be a farmer. [She] is living out her dream." Despite the family tradition of farming, she has changed some things to avoid "pulverizing the land with chemicals and liquid fertilizer," with the goal of "returning the land to a more sustainable state." The farm she owns began as a cotton farm, then switched to soybeans and corn because they were more profitable.

No matter what path a person follows to become a farmer, the support they receive from their family or other farmers is often integral to their success. Rebecca, a 30-year-old white woman who focuses on cheesemaking, explains that the support, both emotional and economic, that she and her husband received from their families made it possible for them to start farming in Georgia sooner than they would have been able to otherwise: "That's a rare story but one that we like telling because we like encouraging people's families to support their children and their grandchildren who want to pursue this kind of a life, because it's really just like starting any other business." In the same way that fishing communities discuss life on the water as making it almost impossible for them to imagine another career, many of the farmers cite a love for farming, seasonality, and the land as what pushed them toward the decision to start farming. Isia, a white urban farmer in Atlanta, explains the reason her family decided to start farming: "Just our love for the land, our need for greater freedom, and our desire to want to be in a place for a long time, a place that we could nurture for a long time. And that desire to create all of that together, I think, is what has really propelled us." Over the course of nine years they have added adjacent land to their urban farm.

Farming, like operating a vineyard or relying on the ocean to fish, is an unpredictable business and extends to becoming a lifestyle choice. Rebecca explains how difficult it is to make cheese professionally: "I still think I'm crazy. I mean, any cheesemaker will tell you it's crazy. You don't do this because it's easy. You don't do this to make money. You do this because there's something about it that you enjoy and love doing. It's a lifestyle choice and it's a hard one." Echoing the shrimpers, who say they could not imagine another life despite the constant hardships, Rebecca's passion for making cheese outweighs any financial risks and hesitations she may have had about entering into such a labor-intensive occupation.

The decision to farm is a reciprocal process that over time evolves into a deeper love and respect for nature in return for the bounty of fresh produce the land produces. Judith, describes how she came to love seasonality:

> The joy of the seasonality it that you get to celebrate things when they're here and then they go away. It's like a family reunion or a homecoming, you don't get to have this thing all the time. You get it this one little special period of time and then you just revel in it until it goes away, but you know it is going to come back.

The love and respect she has for seasonality underscores why she continues to farm and remains faithful to the larger food movement's focus on local produce. As with the families who continue to make a living off the sea, the decision to make a living from the land is often summed up as based on a love and passion for the earth, as Helen, a farmer in Georgia, explains: "I love the soil, I love the earth. And I have always been blessed by what it gave me in return for my love. ... I love the farm."

A love for the land and the desire to enrich one's community frequently intersect on urban farms. Haylene, a black woman in her early forties, describes how growing up in Jamaica shaped her early experiences with farming: "Every one of us have yard space for planting; we might plant a small portion but we normally have large trees, for instance the native breadfruit trees, acai trees, avocado trees ... we don't call it a farm. That's just normal for us." In Jamaica it is not common for women to work—they usually stay home and raise the children—but she followed in her grandparents' footsteps: "Whatever farm DNA is left over from my four grandparents I got all of it, because if I do not farm I'll get sick. ... I have got to put something on the land because I can't live otherwise." Today she is able to feed her entire family from what she grows, and she uses her urban garden as a means to educate people in the community.

The decision to farm and to use organic practices goes beyond being concerned about the environment. It is also sometimes seen as a necessary step in solving chronic health problems. Helen, a white woman in her late seventies, describes her journey into organic food beginning in the 1960s when she was living in Belgium:

> [I] wasn't surprised that I got sick and Nicolas, one year of age, was so sick. So I started changing and I started researching it and it came always down to eating organic. Looking around I couldn't find anything to eat organic. I mean, I could find some dry foods in the local health food store, but I couldn't find anything fresh except my own food which was in the garden. So we started a vegetable garden.

Helen started eating organic when she was 35 years old and has continued to follow organic food practices for over 40 years. When she and her family moved to the United States in 1982, they searched for land to start farming and bought land from a cattle farmer who wanted to retire in Georgia: "The only thing I know is that he never applied chemicals, and he had the land from 1941 until we bought it and he said he never grew much. It was cows all over." Her son has taken over the daily running of the farm and now sells organic produce at the farmers' market and to local restaurants throughout Atlanta.

Even among families with a farming tradition, the decision to focus on organic food in local markets is not always welcomed among the local community. Charlotte's husband's family owns the farm where she works, and the farm has been a whole family endeavor since his father purchased it in 1973: "The whole family is [involved]. Wes's brother, his identical twin, does the grits and the cornmeal and the polenta, and his younger brother helps with the cattle as well. All the family is involved in everything that we do." Although the farm has been in the family for decades, the younger generation has diversified the farm's production from only cattle and hogs to more variety in livestock and crops as well as getting the farm certified as an organic farm amid a growing urban market for such local produce, and despite pushback from the local community. Charlotte explains that a shift is slowly occurring in the community among local farmers that already took place in the Atlanta market: "They are beginning to realize, 'Oh, I don't have to use that. I am just being marketed to.' Then they go back to what their great-grandparents were doing to some degree. It's a little slower to shift in the rural community because they're very set in the way things are." Farmers are forced to balance the consumer demand for local, organic produce with resistance to any new or alternative form of agriculture within the rural farming community.

Although organic farming is often seen as the ideal among small farmers, others are able to find a middle ground between organic and nonorganic practices. Elizabeth, a white woman in her early forties who is a farmer in Mississippi with a large chef clientele, describes her farming practices:

> The bugs have been to a minimum and we aren't spraying for weeds. We are hand-removing them. These are the vegetables my children are eating, that I'm eating, that you're eating, and I feel a responsibility. No, we are not organic, but we try to do the best that we can. You learn to use the weeds in your actual farming practices. We're as responsible as we possibly can be, but we are not organic.

Elizabeth's concern over the chemicals she uses on her farm is reflected in her farming practices. Although organic farming is the ideal shared by most of the farmers, it is not always feasible, and the ability to provide consumers with local food and to remain separate from the industrial agriculture system is as important to them as being certified as fully organic. Environmental concerns also come into play when sourcing a product. Culinary buzzwords such as organic, local, and sustainable have garnered attention in recent years as an alternative to the industrialized food system. Organic, local, and sustainable food is deemed superior in taste to conventional food, if not morally more responsible and superior. The local food trend has replaced organic as a status marker because corporate agriculture has also taken over a large section of the organic market (Deusing, 1996; DeLind, 2000). Chefs and consumers are now turning to local suppliers to reflect their social awareness of product choices. Although local and organic foods are anchored in ethical choices, they also reflect consumers' desire for simple and authentic products (Johnston and Baumann, 2010).

The importance of land goes beyond how the land is treated and extends to what is grown on the land and where the seeds originated. Alisa, a white woman who farms, and her sister sell value-added products at the market. Their family began as sharecroppers in the area over 100 years ago. Although they did not have their own land to farm, vegetables were a source of identity for their family. Alisa explains: "The okra seeds have been in our family about 200 years, passed down from my grandmother from generation to generation. ... It's part of my grandmother, it's your history, and you can't buy it. It wasn't sentimental; it was survival." Historically, feeding a family required a garden that could sustain the family throughout the year, and saving seeds offers a way to preserve memories of the past while existing outside the dominant industrial agriculture structure of society. As sociologist Jennifer Jordan (2015) discusses, saving seeds not only preserves edible memory linked to specific types of produce but also offers an element of food security in being able to save seeds from one year to the next to ensure there will be food on the table in the years to come.

The importance of saving seeds resonates with farmers across the South. Susan, a white woman, explains how the refugees she works with value the seeds of vegetables native to their home country, for example bitter eggplant:

> It's a tradition older than anything; you read in history
> books about people who would put a little baggie of seeds
> in their pocket and carry it over back in the colonial days.
> I find it amazing that families [that] would leave their home
> country with one plastic bag full of stuff will have found a
> way to put some seeds in there.

The tradition of saving seeds is only recently returning to prevalence as seed sourcing concerns become more prominent. Lauren, a Filipino woman in her late twenties who works in Georgia, explains the importance of knowing where her seeds come from:

> It was basically just a shack, and the neighbors of the people
> I was living with at the time were going to get their seeds
> for the fall. ... But there was no way of knowing where they
> came from. They could have come from America. They
> could have come from Monsanto. They could have been
> saved. ... The people really didn't care because that wasn't
> a priority for them. The priority was you have seeds.

Today, she takes pride in the heirloom varieties from the South whose seeds she sources from Southern Exposure Seed Company. Although only one of the farmers mentioned any of the organized seed saving organizations, such as the Seed Savers Exchange, by name, saving seeds or knowing a seed's origin was important to many of the farmers (Carolan, 2011; Jordan, 2015).

As sociologists Sandra Barnes and Benita Blanford-Jones (2019) found in their exploration of black middle-class families in Mississippi, owning land is linked to personal identity and self-worth, as well as future economic stability. Hallie is a 65-year-old African American farmer. She farms land her family has owned for generations. Although the area is historically an African American community, "a lot of blacks left and went north. They either lost their land or sold it." Owning land is very important to Hallie: "If you own your own land, you're really worth something. You can get what you want. You need to at least own your own land, if you can." Owning land becomes a family legacy and a marker of resistance in a region known for not only enslaving generations of African-descended communities but actively working to keep them from owning their own property, developing wealth, and being self-sufficient during the Jim Crow era. The farmers' market offers an opportunity to make a profit off the land while instilling the value of land, gardening, and from-scratch value-added products such as canned and baked goods in younger people.

Although a majority of the farmers in North Carolina and Mississippi are operating farms on family land, for a majority of farmers in Georgia farming is a new adventure on rented land, while others claim empty lots in the middle of segregated cities to create urban farms. Celia, explains the importance of growing food, and of being able to rent land in Georgia to do it:

> Sometimes I think, "Oh, it would be nice to have my own place," but I've come to terms with the reality and really I want to just grow good food and make a living off of it and not be struggling my entire life, which is what I would be doing if I had to buy land of my own.

The financial responsibility of owning land is often too much of a burden for young farmers. Renting land makes it possible to keep the land in agricultural use while reducing some of the financial risk and upfront capital investment. Lauren farms on someone else's land that has been in the same family for over 100 years, she explains the land's transition in the 1970s and 1980s: "Skip's father was doing conventional farming for a little bit on this land. ... As Skip started taking over the farming operation, they converted from a commercial-scale farm into an organic small sustainable farm." Although Skip is now retired from farming, he hires young people, including Lauren, to continue the organic farming tradition he started and helps ensure they are successful by making them pay only for electricity and any improvements they make. Lauren stresses how beneficial this setup is: "Our operating costs are really low. ... That's really the only reason why this is, from a starting point, has made it possible for us to get far and be this successful." Because Celia and Lauren rely on rented land to operate their farms, they are able to grow their businesses without the overhead costs that come with land ownership.

While Celia and Lauren are new to farming and have chosen to live in rural parts of Georgia to run their farms, others have a long agricultural tradition in their families that has survived migration and today thrives in inner-city urban gardens. Cecilia, a 40-year-old black woman, describes the difficulty her parents faced in continuing their traditional food practices when they immigrated from Kenya to the racially segregated inner city of Atlanta: "[My mother] kept a garden for almost a year until people made her afraid of growing food in her own backyard." Cecilia admits that the critics were probably right that it was not safe to grow food in the backyard, because "we don't know what was in the soil when we moved here, it's in the city." Today, she grows food in her front yard and works with her friend Jamila, a fellow gardener, to enhance food production in the West End of Atlanta.

Jamila, a trained environmental engineer and Caribbean immigrant, explains what brought her to the community garden: "If I can't trust what I'm buying at the grocery store and I can't afford whole-paycheck Whole Foods, let me create some access in my community, where I'm living, for the people that need it that can't grow for themselves. I can grow for them." Although many older adults in the community remember a time when almost every family had a small garden, their children are largely divorced from the land and the origins of their food. She continues: "For the most part we go places and we're the only African American farmers, and then part of not many women farmers that are there." The history of race and agriculture in the South is characterized by forced labor, first of slaves and later the sharecroppers of the Jim Crow era. Farming, once a necessity and a forced form of labor, is seen as something to distance oneself from, but in impoverished communities the disappearance of farming traditions is also coupled with a rise in health problems, obesity, and a disconnect from the origins of food. Cecilia and Jamila's urban gardening efforts aim to remedy all three of these problems. Although urban gardens are not without their critics, they offer a degree of food security, especially for those who live in food deserts (Cockrall-King, 2012). The urban gardens operating in the West End of Atlanta have created an affordable option for sourcing healthy foods while also providing a safe place for children and teenagers in the area to spend time after school and an opportunity for them to learn about the origins of their food.

Community

Although farms, with the exception of urban gardens, appear to be isolated plots of land, each with their own house, barn, and equipment, they provide a vital connection to the community and to nature, which was weakened with the rise of industrial agriculture. As Marcie Cohen Ferris (2014) explains, the increasing presence of farmers' markets across the region has created an opportunity for farmers, chefs, and customers to come together once or twice a week around a shared interest in and passion for local food. The result has been the revitalization of seasonal ingredients, foundational to the subsequent increasing popularity of Southern cuisine, yet the specific community dynamics impact the appearance of the local market.

The farmers' market in Greenwood, Mississippi began as part of a larger downtown revitalization project. John, a white man in his late fifties who works as a blueberry farmer, explains that the project aims to

> [B]ring in lots of activities for people to participate in. We are a small agrarian town that doesn't have a lot of entertainment. [The project] has been instrumental in contacting as many farmers as possible. It's one more step in bringing the town to a whole, instead of scattered little pockets and pieces.

The market is located in the middle of town, within walking distance of everything and near the train tracks, the marker of class division within the town limits, making it possible for poor families to walk to the market from the other side of the tracks. The farmers' market emphasizes the relationships farmers have with each other and with their customers. The location of the market has undoubtedly enhanced these relationships. Alisa, a white woman in her mid-fifties, emphasizes the diversity of the town and how the market has brought people together: "The people that come have developed a bond, a friendship. Where it's located is very important. It is located right here on the border and has brought the community—the different cultures in the community together." She explains that the town has both racial and class divides, and the market has brought people together across those lines in a way not seen in other areas of the community. Hal, another white farmer at the market, agrees that the market has created an opportunity for "the poor people around here and the people with the aristocratic roots around here to find a life together that is sustainable, long-term, and of value." The market has provided people with an opportunity to develop relationships across social lines around food, as well as increased access to healthy food options.

The farmers' market is part of a larger social initiative to bridge racial and class gaps in the local community. The farmers' market emphasizes the relationship farmers have to each other and their customers. Alisa, a white woman in her mid-fifties, highlights the diversity of the town and how the market has brought people together: "The people that come have developed a bond, a friendship. Where it's located is very important. It is located right here on the border and has brought the community—the different cultures in the community together." The town has "distinct social class differentiation, not just racial" that the market has brought people together across those lines, even though they "wouldn't ordinarily associate with each other." The market has provided people with an opportunity to develop relationship across social lines. As Alisa mentions: "[It] starts out with food, but it doesn't end with food."

The farmers' market has also provided the opportunity for farmers to try new things while working together and bridging gaps in the community by bridging a relationship between farmers and other market regulars. Hallie, a third-generation black farmer in her mid-sixties, explains: "You get to meet a lot of people. It seems like I am going to see my family when I come to the farmers' market. They all really have become good friends." Leann, a white woman in her mid-fifties, agrees "it is important to know where your food is coming from ... the market also helps to bridge the gap between racial groups." She explains how she benefits because the market provides "an amazing emotional boost, self-esteem, because people are lined up to get the product." Leroy, known as "Spooney," is a local black barbecue cook, sells his products at the market. He explains how relationships have developed between the farmers: "It's more like a family. ... We are like a little family out there and everybody gets along real well." The farmers buy and trade products among themselves, and Spooney is able to "get basically everything [he] needs at the market and doesn't have to go to the grocery store." But he says his favorite things are "the fellowship part, mixing with the people, and the smile they have when they leave."

The relationship between chefs and farmers drives choices across the South. Although there is a close relationship between farmers at the market, chefs and customers who frequent the same stands week after week also develop close relationships with the farmers that can help guide the farmers' choices in what to plant or what breed of livestock to raise. Elizabeth, a white chef and farmer in Mississippi, explains how farming has changed her relationship with food:

> I think for so long we've always known better, but we didn't really do better. It was easy to place that order with Sysco, or it was easy to go to Kroger's and pick up whatever we needed. ... Now it's becoming easier and easier. ... Once you start tasting the difference there is absolutely no turning back.

She now works to educate other chefs about the importance of local food. She loads produce from her farm into her van and travels to Oxford and Memphis to deliver the products each week to chefs at their restaurants: "They've come to count on me just like Sysco, which— they've never had that, and basically like a rolling farmers' market is exactly what I am." Although some chefs frequent the market, others rely on a mobile stand, whereby the farmer delivers directly to the restaurant, ensuring consistent access to fresh produce, in a similar way they rely on Sysco, one of the largest commercial food distribution companies in the United States, to bring produce directly to their door instead of the chef having to go out and search the farmers' market for ingredients.

The relationship between farmers, chefs, and customers has created a unique community at the market in Carrboro, North Carolina that appears very similar to the Mississippi market, but with one major difference: the North Carolina market is located in an affluent college town with longstanding local food traditions. The success of these relationships is rooted in the rules of the markets. Numerous farmers cited the rule that farmers had to sell their own products at the market as something that made it unique. Elise, a white farmer in her mid-thirties who started one of the first community-supported agriculture (CSAs) program in the area and also sells at the market, explains how the rule benefits the customers and the farmers: "I've always really liked that the farmer has to be the seller at the market ... the customer would want that connection with the farmer. ... [There is] a strong knowledge base because the farmers are there." The connection between the farmers and their customers is one of the strongest elements of the market.

Since the farmers are required to sell their own products, they have the opportunity to develop relationships with their customers. The farmers' market provides an opportunity for a community to develop around the shared interests of healthy, local food.

The farmers' market has "cultivated a whole community and culture of folks who care about what they eat, care about the people who grow it, care about their environment, and care about their bodies. ... It has spawned so much good business from a group of farmers coming together," according to Shelia, a 40-year-old white woman who is among the local North Carolina restaurant owners who frequently source produce from the market. Although the social cohesion at the market has strengthened the commitment of farmers, customers, and chefs, it is not without drawbacks. Louise, one of the few black farmers at the North Carolina market, explains: "I don't get to go anyplace. I don't get to have a vacation like I did when I was working because people are always going someplace, or they always got company coming from someplace. And they think you ought to be here [at the market]." Although the rule increases the social solidarity and subsequently positive relationships between vendors, it also means the farmers' market demands a large time commitment from farmers.

The customers at the North Carolina market also include professional chefs who run local restaurants. Shelia runs a restaurant that relies on the farmers' market for products. She finds the relationship between farmers and food interesting, because "it seems like American food now is really being defined by farmers." Bill, a white man in his mid-sixties and another local restaurant owner, describes his relationship with the market in a similar way: "Our menu is not fixed. I always go [to the market] and see what there is and that is what we [cook]." As Ferris (2014) explains in her work on Southern food culture, the market is known for the direct relationship between farmers and chefs, with chefs pushing for more diverse products at the market.

The North Carolina farmers' market has changed and grown over time. Wilma, a white woman, has been at the market since the beginning. She explains the changes in the community of the market as a product of the changes in size: "It was almost a family get-together every Saturday. ... Now there are a lot more people, a lot more vendors, and many more customers." Louise, who sells baked goods she makes from scratch, notes the relationship between the vendors. Although there are a lot of vendors, "none of [them] are making—doing the same thing, so there isn't any competition. ... [They] all get along really well." The market's ability to continue to change by accepting new, noncompeting vendors has contributed to its long-term success.

Although Ben and Karen, a white couple in their mid-fifties, both trained at the Culinary Institute of America, their cooking styles are rooted in their childhood experiences. Ben did not grow up on a farm, but his grandparents maintained a garden throughout his childhood and other family members were tobacco farmers with gardens for subsistence farming. His family emphasized the importance of "being together [that meant] being together at the table." Those childhood meals "drove a lot of my thinking about how to eat in a sort of seasonal way because it was always seasonal. What was in the yard was what we were eating." Not only was he exposed to the importance of food at a young age, but his grandmother also spent time instructing him on how to cook. Karen also grew up around food. Her grandparents "grew the food, put it on the plate ... life totally revolved around food." At a young age she realized that food could impress people and make them happy. This link between memory and taste plays out across home and commercial kitchens as chefs seek out the taste memories that link their food to a specific place and time (Jordan, 2015).

The farmers in Georgia are not all linked to the same farmers' market, although most participate in markets across the Atlanta area. They do not share the same underlying goals and rules that the Mississippi and North Carolina markets rely on to guide motivations and interactions. Jenny, describes the area around her Georgia farm:

> At least in this part of the county [it] is very undeveloped. There is still a lot of open farmland. So it is nice to ride through the county and see the same families that have owned big tracts of land are still holding onto that land. You know, they may not be farming it organically or intensively like we do but it is nice to see that people still value land and that we have kind of a buffer from the development. ... I would love to see more small diversified farms because obviously there is a demand for it. We have over 100 people that have signed up on our waiting list for a CSA and so it's a dream to see more younger people move into the area and start farming food again.

The demand for local fruits and vegetables has made it possible for more young people to seriously consider farming as an occupation. Although the push for organic and sustainable farms is largely a white middle-class demand that is still met with resistance in rural areas, the increasing demand is often great enough to overcome this resistance.

Although the success of farmers' markets increases consumer demand, it does not always translate to an increased demand or general awareness of local food in rural areas. Helen explains the difficulty of establishing a sense of community amid the resistance to organic produce: "What I understand the community is—the people around us, who live close to us, nobody takes our veggies from around us. They're not interested. So, all the community is in Atlanta. When you say community for me it's really not here, it's out there." This sentiment was echoed by farmers across the Southeast. Although they had found a market for their products in the urban centers and farmers' markets, there was still resistance or complete avoidance from their neighbors, who were more accustomed to conventional farming practices and shopping at grocery stores even though they live in areas surrounded by farms.

Urban farmers in Georgia have had more success in connecting with the local community than those in rural areas. Judith, explains how she understands what farming and nature offer for her life:

> You can enrich an entire community. ... Relationship was key, and being able to have a genuine and authentic relationship with [nature] as much as our lives as possible. Our work being meaningful and authentic, what we eat being meaningful and authentic and the people that surround us—farming is able to give you all of that.

Although Judith recognizes that other farmers, especially those in rural areas, have had more difficulty getting local community members to buy in, those in urban areas such as Atlanta have benefited from the increasing awareness of the local food movement common among their highly educated and well-resourced clientele. The ability to strengthen a community through a connection with nature plays out across urban farms, as Isia, a white woman in her mid-thirties, explains:

> I think that's what we yearn for, we yearn for something that is more entrenched in our community and our community values, like knowing your neighbor. What helps sustain those things are these small markets, this coming out, talking to your farmer, all of these little daily rituals that create that smaller sense of community.

Isia describes the importance of small urban farms for the development of community and the overall food movement in Atlanta. As with the wineries that operate U-picks as part of their farms and community events to bring people into contact with nature, many farmers are working toward the same goal of strengthening community awareness of nature, especially regarding how the food system operates.

Race, gender, and class

Farming as a profession faces the same inequalities that plague many other industries. The South has a complicated history regarding farming and race, class, and gender, with the poor and people of color often working as sharecroppers for upper-class whites or struggling to survive on their own land (Barnes and Blanford-Jones, 2019). Today, farmers are no longer only the older white men wearing overalls. Instead, women and young families are now entering into farming as a profession. Although historically women have played a significant role in societal agricultural practices, the shift to industrial agriculture also paralleled a shift in gender roles, with women being responsible for household tasks that no longer included tending a garden (Coontz, 2006; Engelhardt, 2011).

There is a recent resurgence in women becoming farmers, but they continue to struggle to be seen as legitimate farmers by their customers as well as with the balance between working and motherhood. Although Isia has faced some pushback because she has only been farming for about ten years, she explains that age isn't the main problem she faces: "I think for me as a woman farmer, it's been a little more of a struggle. I think a lot of time people in their mind, when they think of the term farmer, they think of the old white man." She gives the example of her interactions with a customer at the farmers' market: "I've even had a man say to me, 'Well, you're too pretty to be a farmer.' I'm like, 'Well, buddy, you are in shock because I know like 30 gorgeous women farmers and some of them even wear lipstick on their tractor.'" Women farmers are often greeted with initial skepticism even when they are part of a larger family farming enterprise. Jenni, a white woman in her mid-twenties, describes the pushback she gets initially from customers at the Georgia market because she is a woman farmer:

> People don't expect for me to say "my farm," and probably 50 percent will come back and say "your farm?" But I consider that a blessing because then I get to say, "Yes ma'am, that was grown on my farm." I'm actually the

fifth generation and we've been on the same piece of land since 1866.

Although many women farmers have difficulties with customers, they do not face the same skepticism from within the farming community, where shared labor and knowledge is often enough to be seen as a legitimate participant in the profession.

Some landowners even encourage women farmers by renting land to them. Lauren, explains how the landowner where she farms in Georgia sees the importance of women farmers: "Skip has said to me that he thinks women are the best farmers because we have that natural tendency to be mothers and to nurture things. And that's really what farming is, you are nurturing plants." She elaborates on why she thinks women make the best farmers: "Women have a deeper connection to food. ... Overall there are more women that cook every day in their homes and that are home cooks and that pickle and can and cook for their children." For Lauren, the passion for and connection to food and family is another aspect of farming.

The connection between nurturing farms and families is a recurring theme among women farmers. As Rebecca, a 30-year-old white woman, notes:

> I think that for a lot of women there is this inherent need to nurture and this inherent disposition to nurture and this inherent connection to land. I think that we have as women kind of pushed away from that because it was in many ways forced on us. And it's really lovely that women are coming back to it but on their own terms.

She describes the history of cheesemaking as traditionally a dreaded part of women's household labor because it was long, tiring work but necessary for survival. However, she sees people, especially women, coming back to farming and cheesemaking today because it is no longer about survival but is now a choice women can make, to engage in these traditional practices and sell their products as a stable business model. As Richard Ocejo (2017) found among craft producers in New York, jobs that were traditionally seen as low status are now viable options for young educated adults seeking an alternative to traditional office work across the South.

Susan, a white woman, helped start a farm project for refugees in Georgia. She describes her initial surprise when working with women from Burundi, who are culturally responsible for growing food to feed their families while the men are responsible for working on commercial farms for income:

> These women would identify children and growing food at the same value level of who they were. ... In our society, which has lost a lot of—and certainly we're trying to recover it—but has lost a lot of connection to a local food economy, where our food comes from, to how local food systems work, these people are experts who live and breathe and only know how to function when they can grow their own food, preserve their own foods, feed their families.

Although nurturing the land is an important aspect of women farmers' motivation, for some the link between farming and children is so intertwined that it becomes foundational to their identity as women and as mothers.

For women farmers who have this focus on land and motherhood, they work to incorporate their children into the farming practices as educating the next generation becomes an essential part of their work. Charlotte, a white woman in her early forties, explains how her perspective on farming has changed since her seven-year-old son began accompanying her around their Georgia farm: "He does everything. He works with me. ... Becoming a mother, again, I think drives it even deeper that we really have to do what we do. We have to do this work. ... It's not just for us. It's for the next seven generations." Although she hopes her son will eventually take over the farm, her goal is to instill sustainable agricultural practices that will ensure the farm's success and continued operation for many generations to come. The desire to educate children, whether their own or those in the community, becomes an important aspect of farming. Cecilia, explains: "I think the bigger piece is that we are invested in seeing our communities grow and be connected to this experience. We can't have our kids running from chickens and calling goats dogs and asking us whether we can grow cheese in the soil." The distance between farms and food limits many children's and adults' understanding of where food comes from. Haylene describes an experience she had while giving children a tour of the farm:

> I asked them where do the different vegetables come from and they called out the name of a supermarket. ... I have had grown people that have never seen what a tomato plant

looked like. The grown ones might be able to tell you this is a tomato, but as far as they are concerned the tomato came from the supermarket.

Haylene grew up around nature and sees farming as an integral part of her life. Today she uses her urban farm in Georgia to educate others, especially children, about the origins of food.

Although many women farmers emphasize the link between farming and family, for others finding that balance is more difficult. Celia and her husband run a farm in Georgia, but the work–life balance became more challenging when their son was born: "It has been the greatest challenge, it's incredibly rewarding but it's been very difficult for me in the last year balancing keeping the farm going and meeting all of my son's needs." For her, reducing the amount of time she spent manning the farm's stand at the market every weekend offered a partial solution to spending more time with her family and maintaining her farm. Women farmers, as with women who work outside the home, are forced to negotiate childcare as well as pushback from their customers in historically male-dominated professions. As Michael Borer (2019) found among women craft brewers, while small in number, their knowledge and skill set commands respect from their male counterparts, but whether through branding and market imagery or consumer assumptions, women still face challenges in the field.

These challenges exacerbate other aspects of promoting farming, family, and healthy food options among women. Kate Cairns and Josee Johnston (2015) found in their research on how women negotiate everyday food concerns that, contrary to popular beliefs that the desire for local, organic food is isolated to the middle and upper classes, a desire for healthy food is pervasive in modern society, but access remains limited, often due to monetary constraints. Most families—and especially mothers, who remain overwhelmingly responsible for their children's diets and health—constantly work to put healthy food on the table, but time, access, and finances often make health secondary to ensuring that children are at least eating (Bowen, Brenton, and Elliot, 2019).

Although health was a motivating factor in the North Carolina market, it was a secondary issue in the Mississippi market. Like other towns, the one in Mississippi is becoming more health-conscious and looking for local food, but the creation of the farmers' market was part of a larger town-wide revitalization project. Hal, a white man in his late fifties, argues that the shift to sustainability has occurred because "it has just become the buzzword." The market makes it easier for customers to interact with the farmers. John, a white man in his late fifties, explains that the market gives customers the opportunity to ask the farmers questions regarding how the produce was grown and also how to cook the products. The products sold at the market "provide health-conscious people with the blueberries, but there are just as many that eat them, not because of the health but because of the good taste. They just love the flavor." Donald, a white man in his mid-forties who owns a bakery and sells his products at the market, recognizes the importance of the market and the shift in local preferences regarding food: "It is also a great selling point and it ties it all in together and people are interested in trying it." He explains that it took time to convince people that local products were better, and he uses seasonal products purchased from the market to make his breads.

The Mississippi based farmers' market is unique because one of the goals is to ensure the products are available to people of diverse social groups. Hallie, a black woman in her mid-sixties, explains the voucher system: "a lot of peoples couldn't afford what they wanted. The vouchers help a lot of people. People that have a low income [and the elderly] get them." Hallie also makes an effort to get produce to those with mobility issues: "Old people are not able to come here, so I have to deliver stuff to them." Farmers' markets provide opportunities to alleviate community issues such as promoting healthy, local foods through cost-effective measures and working with existing policies to support families from many backgrounds, not simply the ones who have always afforded these products.

Although the Mississippi market opened with the explicit goals of improving social cohesion in the local community and revitalizing the area, most farmers are left to their own devices to decide how to improve the community and what they wish to pursue. Haylene explains how the history of the Maroons, an enslaved group of people brought over from Africa who were able to survive and gain freedom, connects to her personal history and her love of gardening:

> They did not listen to a slave master and they were thrown off the boat and left to die or survive. And survive they did. It's a lot of history about the Maroon culture, similar to the Geechee Gullah people. That's all along the water coast, there are groups of people that inhabited the island and that's when I say it is in my DNA—farming and fishing were their survival, and hunting. I would really love if our people would take more interest in farming or gardening or learning to produce for themselves to sustain themselves

with healthy food. ... If 10 percent of the people, especially
in the West End, decides to plant a garden they will be able
to feed all the others.

She shares her passion for farming with others in her community in
the racially segregated and impoverished West End of Atlanta.

Despite the success of small-scale and local farmers' markets, there
is still a gap in access. Jenni, a white woman, describes the type of
customer that frequents her family's Georgia business: "We quickly
found out that our customer is anybody that has a high amount of
disposable income, a person who has studied the food production
system and understood and demanded something different, done by
hand, done locally, done sustainably." Her business traditionally focused
on grass-raised cattle and eventually added sheep, goats, chickens, and
other livestock in addition to an organic vegetable farm and pastured
eggs. Although urban community gardens, such as Haylene's, are
rooted in the local community in a way that farmers' markets are not,
the question of access and affordability resonates across the South
as markets continue to pop up in major urban areas such as Atlanta
or affluent college towns such as Chapel Hill. While the Mississippi
market was focused on community revitalization and providing access
for every member of the community, that model is not the dominant
one across the region.

The underlying founding purpose of the North Carolina and
Mississippi farmers' markets coincides with larger community projects
dedicated to healthy food, community cohesion, and either new or
continued revitalization. The North Carolina market, located in
a historically affluent and progressive college town, is just another
expression of the larger community ethos that permeates its activities
and vibrant art scene. It is in this context that the healthy and local
food provided by the market makes its way to consumers, either to
be cooked at home or to grace the plates at one of the many local
farm-to-table restaurants.

The Mississippi market is located in a once thriving agrarian
community filled with cotton growers that declined throughout
the 20th century as cotton production was mechanized and boll
weevils decimated crops. During the 1960s the small town was at
the center of numerous Civil Rights activities including the March
Against Fear in 1966. Today the town is largely racially segregated by
the railroad tracks that once saved the town by providing a way to
move products from the cotton factories to far-off destinations, and
revitalization or gentrification efforts have renovated several buildings

downtown as well as brought in the typical markers of a gentrifying neighborhood: boutique hotels, art galleries, and eclectic restaurants (Zukin, 1981; Sarmiento, 2020). It is within this context that the farmers' market, as a tool of revitalization, was founded in 2008. Although the market maintains the mission of providing healthy food for everyone, the larger citywide context and continuing gentrification cannot be ignored (Alkon, Kato, and Sbicca, 2020).

The Georgia farmers present a slightly different story of the connection between farming and place. These farmers do not all sell together at the same market, although some of them do know each other. They are more critical of their neighbors' lack of receptiveness to local and organic food than of the Atlanta based markets where they sell their products, which reflects historical understandings of organic food as a high-priced luxury product with origins in the alternative lifestyle culture found in California in the 1960s (Kauffman, 2018).

Taken together, these three distinct farmers' markets shed light on the community dynamics and broader understanding of the question "healthy food for whom?" to elucidate the relationship between space and community. Although willing to sell their product to everyone in need of healthy food, these farmers and the farmers' markets are constrained by the underlying inequalities and gentrification trends that privilege the middle- and upper-class consumers who have an existing awareness of the local food movement (Romero and Harris, 2019). However, the urban farms in Atlanta present an interesting counterpoint by providing low-income communities, often ignored by the typical farmers' market, with a space in which to learn and experience local food while simultaneously addressing questions of food insecurity and farming traditions. Despite these differences, all the farmers exist within the broader context of the South and its accompanying traditions and innovations.

Southern traditions

April, a white farmer in North Carolina, explains that the relationship she has with customers includes the stories and history behind the food, and these various parts are all "as much a part of [her] product line or mission as a business as just selling the product." The identity of the market balances the relationships between farmers and customers with a desire to maintain the Southernness that is unique to the area. Although the area "[has a] lack of Southernness because of the population ... [she] didn't want to lose those things." April used her interest in maintaining a Southern identity to shape her choices about what products to grow and sell in order to connect with the heritage embedded in the region's foodways.

Authenticity and originality play an important role in the success vendors have at the market. Alex, a white man in his mid-fifties, discusses the importance of being authentic: "Customers are going to come and buy from those folks they think are the ones telling them the real story about the product. They are going to want to know particularly if it is your family product." The story behind the product is an important aspect of selling it to customers, and this includes being able to answer questions regarding where the seeds came from, how they were grown, and the best way to cook the product. Alex continues: "To be authentic and original is harder and harder to do but there are specialties to get into." It is through the perfection of specific products that farmers are able to be successful.

Being original and authentic is achieved through the diversity of products as well as remaining true to conceptualizations of what it means to produce Southern food. Bill, who has a local farm-to-table restaurant, explains how the spirit of Southern food is linked to the nostalgia of "what grandmamma cooked. Part of homemaking was cooking ... it was in the home and it was a seasonal thing. It is framed by the culture of the South, which is the things that grow here and the history of the region and who was here." Michael, a white farmer, identifies Southern food as a combination of "the staple Southern items—corn, peas, butter beans, greens, and sweet potatoes—[with] a lot of crops that I did not even know what they were two or three years ago ... like kale and kohlrabi." Diversity and nostalgia make it possible for farmers to meet customer demand for new products while remaining true to the demands for authenticity in Southern food through the products they sell. Marjorie has grown a variety of products because "Southerners love their greens and cornbread and fried chicken." Despite her experience with traditional Southern products, she recognizes the importance of growing products that are healthy even though they are not historically identified with the South, such as Jerusalem artichokes.

Bill, who helped start the farmers' market, explains the balance between authenticity and originality: "The market started out just growing the traditional stuff ... then with time there began to be a demand for those strange things that nobody had." Over time, the variety of products has increased. Sarah, the market manager, highlights the increase in diversity in terms of both produce and value-added products: "A lot of folks are really pushing themselves to grow specialty products."

Value-added products are nearly synonymous with Southern farmers' markets today. Alisa, a white woman in her mid-fifties, explains that their garden is the source of all of the products that they can and sell at the market. The garden has given Alisa and her sister the chance to deepen their relationship because the products they make are from recipes passed down from their mother and grandmother: "Everything we make, somebody in the family tastes. When people ask about our products, I take a great deal of pride in—and I tell them the story. ... I want them to know they're buying something from somebody that enjoyed making it." April is a vendor at the North Carolina market. She sells pickles, preserves, and baked goods and sources most of her produce from local farmers who "had excess produce but neither had the extended family, or the labor for people, or the skill of how to preserve and put up those products ... to do value-added products." Despite April's passion for value-added products, she describes the problem of convincing her mother of their value: "People can make their own preserves. [Her mother is] still very much a part of the culture that devalues women's work that is handmade or homemade, they take it for granted. They value it but not in a monetary state." There is a generational resistance to revaluing domestic labor. Marjorie is an 81-year-old farmer who labels herself a housewife: "I go to the farmers' market carrying vegetable, flowers, and fruit. Otherwise I am a housewife." She not only reduces her own responsibilities and roles to those of a housewife, but she does not see the value in value-added products: "In the long run I'm afraid [value-added products] are not going to be a good thing." Marjorie sees the relationship between traditional women's labor, such as canning or pickling, as something women should be doing at home, not selling, because it does not translate into monetary value since anyone can do it, instead the focus should be on raw products.

Yet other consumers see value-added products as facilitating the consumption of taste memories among consumers who no longer have the skill or knowledge to can their own pickles and jams or bake their own bread from scratch. Although there are generational gaps in understanding the value in value-added products, there is a recognition of the need to educate younger people about the value behind farming and value-added products. Louise, an African American woman, is a baker who only cooks from scratch using local products. She explains that "[baking from scratch] is a lost art ... and we are losing a lot of art and heritage. If the younger people don't do it then we won't have anybody." Louise sees baking from scratch, a traditional form of domestic labor, as an art form that should be valued as art. Baking from scratch is described as a valuable skill and knowledge, not an exploitive source of profit. Alisa agrees, describing canning as "a dying art" that must be passed down to be preserved.

These discussions around value-added products extend across the South, but the success of the Southern wine industry is now translating to other agricultural products including cheese. Rebecca, a cheesemaker from Georgia, explains how the same rhetoric used in the wine industry is beginning to impact cheesemaking in positive ways: "I'm not an expert in terroir but I think people like the idea of being able to put a little piece of where they live in their mouth and experiencing—that is becoming more and more important to folks." Although the South does not have a long tradition of cheesemaking, the rising demand for local products has increased the number of cheesemakers in the region, and as they refine their technique, more Southern cheesemakers are winning national awards for their products. Rebecca discusses how important the return of small-scale agriculture is in Georgia, and in the South in general:

> This renaissance of farming that we're experiencing is really—I feel like it's 20 years behind other places like Vermont. ... I mean, everybody in Vermont has a CSA share. It's an institution. Here people still have no idea what a CSA is, but there are people who do and it's growing year by year. It's a really exciting place to be, to see that growth happening and see people waking up to it. ... Once you have a tomato that tastes like a tomato you can't go back to eating those water hydroponic things that they're growing in South America. That's definitely helped move this movement along, is that once you know you can't un-know.

The connection to a Southern identity is only one facet of the multitude of considerations influencing a person's decision to start a small-scale farm, what type of products they grow, and what practices they employ. Yet these decisions have real-time consequences for consumers who rely on farmers' markets for local produce or the edible memories embedded in heirloom tomatoes or strawberry jam.

Conclusion

Farmers' markets are not a new phenomenon, but their popularity has increased dramatically in the past 20 years. The South has always been known for its farm stands, little stops on the side of the road that appear in the summer and boast large quantities of local peaches, watermelon, and corn, then disappear again as the season ends. The market that stays open year round, with a variety of locally grown produce, grass-fed meats, and value-added baked and canned goods, is relatively new, increasing in popularity as a generation whose grandparents and great-grandparents relied on small subsistence farms and canned products to make it through winter, wars, and the Great Depression begin to demand those same products and seek an alternative to industrial agriculture. The juxtaposition between organic and local, urban and rural, and produce and value-added products offers three spaces where Southern farmers and farmers' markets are forced to negotiate what it means to be a community-oriented business in the modern South. This negotiation fits into the ongoing process of impression management that is constantly evolving as "craft" becomes a common household phrase.

Although it is easy to see how value-added products at a farmers' market fit into popular conceptualizations of craft, there is a need to broaden the understanding of a craft product beyond something that has been created by hand, such as homemade jams and preserves, to include the people responsible for creating the original raw material, which sheds light on how these products come to exist. As Heather Paxson (2013) has shown in her work with artisanal cheesemakers, they cannot separate their cheese from the animals they raise: the final product and the raw material exist on the same farm and must be cared for simultaneously to produce the final product. Although many other products are not as closely linked, a craft beer, artisanal bread, or local butcher shop would not exist without the farmers who grow and raise the raw materials that go into these finished products.

Although less glamorous than the craft cocktail bar tucked into a corner in New York City described by Richard Ocejo (2017) or the craft breweries dotting the Las Vegas landscape in Michael Borer's (2019) work, farmers play a significant role in both these contexts, from growing the mint and cherries that are muddled into a craft cocktail to growing the hops that will one day become beer. These professions are not new, as many of the farmers featured in this chapter grew up in families with longstanding farming traditions. The understanding of craft products needs to encompass not only the glamourous or exclusive experiences and purveyors in major urban areas but also the knowledge and artistry of the farmers who care for the raw ingredients.

The decision to farm, and the commitment to farming, often using organic or almost organic methods, is of great importance to farmers who are seeking out the connection between produce and the land. For many the taste memories, or edible memory, embedded in specific produce, whether from seeds saved and brought across the ocean or the memory of homemade jams and jellies from produce raised in a kitchen garden, motivate the current generation of farmers to provide others with these same taste memories (Jordan, 2015; Abarca, 2017). These taste memories resonate across Southern foodways, remaining deeply embedded in the food traditions of the region and extending to new generations of consumers beyond the confines of the South.

4

Smokehouses: The Art of Curing Meats

One early January afternoon in 2016, flames erupted from the Edwards Virginia Smokehouse, causing $2.5 million worth of ham and sausage, as well as the buildings and three generations of history, to burn to the ground. In 2019, the family that owns Edwards, the third generation in a business opened in the 1920s along the banks of the James River in Surry, Virginia, just across the river from Jamestown, still had not rebuilt. Although the business is still operating through a succession of other people's smokehouses in North Carolina, Kentucky, and Missouri, the farm-to-table chain the Edwards family had created around their ham products had not been rebuilt. The family sourced local heritage breed pigs raised on a specific peanut feeding system unique to the Virginia region where the original smokehouse was located, and where peanut farmers are plentiful; however, without the Surry smokehouse the cost of shipping pigs from Virginia to other states is prohibitive. Almost three years after the fire, the first batch of Surryano ham, the most iconic of Edwards products, was released, but it is not the same. The unique aspect of dry-aged or cured country ham is the specific combination of bacteria and yeast present in each smokehouse; it is the terroir of the country ham business that makes each brand unique. The popularity of Surryano ham extended far beyond the Tidewater region of Virginia: it featured prominently on the menus of award-winning restaurants in Washington, DC, and New York City, including David Chang's Momofuku (Stolberg, 2016; Korfhage, 2019).

The Edwards fire occurred three years after the largest country ham producer in Virginia and one of the largest in the United States, Smithfield, was bought by a Chinese company. This international purchase followed a series of consolidations that brought most of the Surry and Smithfield area country ham producers into the giant

Smithfield conglomerate, which is known for its unique Smithfield hams that are protected under Virginia law in the same way that Greek feta is in Europe. In 2018, the company completely closed down its country ham production and smokehouse (Schneider, 2018). Thus, another legacy in Southern foodways was relegated to the memories of those who had the chance to taste a heritage craft product.

Although the process of curing began out of necessity as a way to preserve meat before the advent of refrigeration, those same methods continue to be practiced across Tennessee, Kentucky, Virginia, and North Carolina today. Preserving meats, especially ham, is an art form passed down from the colonial era in the US. However, despite the current financial success and popularity of select companies known for their hams, these families turned to curing meats because it was a way to make money in tight financial times, and as with the Edwards family, many continue to struggle. In a region known for its farming communities, cured hams and other specialty cuts of meat have survived changing consumer demand without losing touch with the flavors and traditions that make these products unique. This chapter explores the evolution, and at times controversial meaning, of country ham in North Carolina, Virginia, Tennessee, and Kentucky. In these states country ham is a way of life, often finding its place on holiday tables across the region and into the kitchens of award-winning restaurants in major urban areas. Yet the focus is not on chefs such as David Chang who choose to feature these products on their menus, but on the current generation of families who produce country hams across the South.

The evolution of country ham

Prior to the advent of refrigeration, curing was one of the only ways to preserve meats for the entire year. Cured meats often reflected the game or livestock available in a region. When colonists first landed at Jamestown, the Indigenous people were already curing wild game, and the colonists took the techniques they learned from the Indigenous people and applied it to the pigs they had brought with them. By 1750, peanut fed hams were being shipped to England by Virginia farmers (Edge, 2017).

The process of curing meats dates back to ancient times and has fundamentally remained the same. June, one of the few women curemasters, describes some of the ancient history surrounding cured hams:

> Some of the earliest writings was written by a fellow named
> Cato. ... One of the things he described was how to process

a country ham. He didn't exactly call it a country ham, he just said to cure the ham you put it in a jar and cover it with salt and let it set for about 40 days, which is exactly what we do. ... Then he said take it out and wash it and hang it in the air to dry. Now this was equivalent to the equalization process—that's what you are trying to do is dry it down in equalization—and he said do that for another ten days, which is exactly what we do. And [that] was written several hundred years before Christ.

The historical process she describes is very general, but it dates back centuries. As June explains, her curing process is very similar to the original processes she has read about in history books.

Although the process of curing meats in general is ancient, the regional history of country hams began when English settlers arrived in Jamestown. Sam, the current head of the Edwards family business, explains:

There's an island in Surry called Hog Island, directly across from Jamestown Island where the settlers that came from England brought the pigs from England and put them on this island because of its natural barriers, and they were allowed to forage in the forest, and they could survive. And then whenever the settlers needed a pig they would row across, slaughter the animal, bring him back, have a big barbecue, and dry-cure the rest. Now I'm speculating a little bit there, but that's the story that's been passed down along with the American Indian, the influence that they had on dry-curing wild game.

He is describing the local lore about how cured ham became commonplace, first in colonial Virginia and then into the modern era. Sam is the third generation of the Edwards family to produce country ham. When his grandfather started the business, he called the hams Wigwams as a tribute to the history of the region and the Indigenous people who had shared their knowledge and techniques with the colonists.

Although the preservation of meat, specifically country ham, can be traced throughout the colonial period, the process evolved over time to become more consistent through the implementation of new technologies. A country ham relies on the four seasons to be cured in a way that replicates the terroir of the place and tradition.

However, modern health codes demand that it is done in a sealed room, allowing for precise temperature controls to duplicate the seasons instead of relying on the whims of Mother Nature. Sam describes the changes that have occurred in curing since his grandfather started the business: "Back in the day when my grandfather did it, the major difference is Mother Nature was providing the humidity and the temperatures. I'm talking about in 1926." When his father took over the business in the 1950s, he implemented a controlled temperature system. The controlled system ensures that the product is the same each year and is not vulnerable to extreme weather changes.

Rufus, a second generation curemaster in North Carolina, explains how the curing process changed over time, focusing on when his father first came to the company that Rufus now manages in the 1970s:

> What they did up in the mountains was ambient curing. So, it was not controlled—and when Dad got down here—and the ham industry was having a lot of trouble because they were trying to equalize hams. You know, all we're doing is reproducing the seasons: the salt room in wintertime when the hogs were killed on the farm; spring—and then they would go through the springtime temperatures, which is around 50 to 60. And then they go through the summertime heat, and then the farmers would usually cut the hams in the fall of the year. The ham industry was missing the—when Dad came down here, they were missing the—the middle stage, the equalization. They were trying to do everything in the salt room, and it was not getting up to the proper temperature. ... Dr. Bloomer and Dr. Christian up at NC State [University], they were the ones that were instrumental in coming up with the middle stage, the equalization room.

Rufus, although not a business owner, is the plant manager for a North Carolina based country ham company and is continuing the traditions his father started. The use of new technologies has stabilized the curing process. While smokehouses are still vulnerable to fire, new technologies at least eliminate the once-common risk of losing a year's worth of product because of too much rain in the spring or too extreme temperatures.

While technology makes it possible to more easily regulate the curing process, many producers are still quite selective in how they adapt to the new methods. Charles, Jr., a second generation curemaster known for his bacon and country ham products, explains:

We use two smokers at a time to smoke our bacon and it usually takes two rounds of that. So normally it's 96 hours of smoking to get us the color. ... Probably one smoking would give us the smoke flavor but we're after the color and the appearance of an old-fashioned quality product ... we haven't changed the original methods that were done back before the days of refrigeration.

His Kentucky curing business still relies on the process implemented by his father during the 1940s, although unlike his father, he is not as dependent on the changes in the weather that could cause his father to lose an entire year's worth of product.

Although the curing process is relatively consistent across country ham producers, there are slight variations in style or flavoring beyond the terroir offered by the curing house itself that make the final product unique. Ron, the second-generation owner of his family's Virginia-based cured ham business, explains what country ham means to him:

Here locally, country ham would be sugar-cured. There's a lot of different styles. There's smoked, there's salt-cured, there's some cured where they add a lot of pepper. But ours use a brown sugar, salt, and a little bit of saltpeter, which is sodium nitrate, as a preservative. The most common comment I hear is it tastes like what my grandfather used to cure on the farm. So, people come in and they have that—it's like it brings back a lot of memories and we're not going to try to change that.

Although his grandfather began curing meat as a way to preserve it because there was no refrigeration available at the time, the flavor became popular and continues to be sought out by consumers because of its ability to create taste memories (Abarca, 2017).

In the same way Southern wine is known for the region and for specific grapes, such as the muscadine grape unique to the Carolinas, country ham represents a place as much as it does the process behind the product, grounding it and its producers in the world of craft products. Sydney, a Virginia restaurant owner, describes how he thinks of the regionality behind country ham:

The ham belt was right across the Memphis bridge into the northern part of Arkansas but before you got to the Ozarks. So probably about 20 to 30 miles in, and then you'd come across and you'd swoop down—even the Delta of Mississippi was a big pig area. And you'd go down as far as almost Jackson and swing up by Greenville and usually it was on this side of Highway 55 but then ventured over into Oxford a little bit and then straight up to the north and would cover across the northern part of Alabama and Tennessee and Virginia. When Virginia was doing hams, it wasn't really up in the northern part. It was more down in the southern part, and that's why I call it a belt. Now they do it everywhere because everybody has learned the techniques and with modern society and tool[s] and stuff you can do it just about anywhere. I mean, but even up in Wisconsin, and all they're pig people but there are these spots where it is not so that's why I call that the Southern belt.

Sydney grew up in Mississippi watching his father and grandfather cure hams each winter. Today, he has a small smokehouse behind his restaurant where he continues the tradition of curing ham, but instead of being a family endeavor, the final product is sold in his restaurant.

Although country ham is uniquely Southern, it is similar to the cured meats of Europe such as prosciutto and Serrano pork products. Sam, the third generation in his family's country ham business, explains:

> I think if you look at the globe, you'll see that Virginia, Kentucky, Tennessee, North Carolina is between the latitudes that produce well-cured meat. If you look at Italy and Spain and Germany, which in that part of the world they're known for the product, they have dry-cured meats. We have the same weather patterns here.

The major difference between the American and European markets is the absence of strict regulations on what can be produced where. Sam compares ham to the wine industry, which is controlled by place-specific production guidelines in Europe that do not exist in the US:

> I think what it boils down to in a sense is like the wine industry. You buy chardonnay from X, Y, Z company in California, one in Missouri, and one in Virginia, they're all chardonnays but they all taste different. You buy it because you like the way that guy does it, and I think that's true with country ham.

Sam explains the differences in regulation between country ham producers, who do not have the established industry standards to guide their production in the way European prosciutto and Serrano producers do. This leads to more variety across products each suited to a different taste palate. However, country ham, as with American wine, is equal to its European counterparts, although it does not have the same historical respect. While the Judgement of Paris changed perceptions of California wines, the success of country ham within the current artisanal food movement is increasing the respect consumers have for the American versions of these iconic European meats.

The technology of the curing process behind country ham has changed dramatically since the colonists first learned how to cure meat from the Indigenous communities, but the core of the process is the same. The seasons, whether generated by Mother Nature or a temperature controlled room, produce the unique taste that makes it known as country ham. This process facilitates the connection between the product, which is embedded with authenticity through the year-long curing process dating back centuries, and the taste memories reflecting previous generations' employment of the same process. More recently, country ham producers have sought the return of something nearly lost to time to replicate some of the earliest iterations of American country ham: heritage breed pigs.

Heritage breed pigs

John T. Edge points out the inaccuracy of the popular belief that the process of Southern barbecue, in all its regional variations, was more important than the raw product that went into it. From this perspective it was up to the barbecue pitmaster, the artisan, to use his or her skills and knowledge to create the final product. The early 2000s saw a subtle shift in this philosophy as barbecue pitmasters began seeking out heritage breed pigs with higher fat content. Thus, the art involved in barbecue changed slightly because the raw ingredients changed (Edge, 2017). The shift to heritage breeds was part of a broader increased awareness and concern regarding industrial agriculture and the superior taste of livestock and vegetables raised outside that system (Jordan, 2015). Although these products are generally more expensive, at times prohibitively such as in the case of small barbecue restaurants, they reflect a time when curing ham was done by the same farmer who raised the pig. The evolving consumer demand for locally sourced and artisanal products makes it possible for producers to return to these heritage breeds.

Allan, a Tennessee based country ham producer who started making country ham after realizing his salary as a guidance counselor was not enough, explains how he began curing country ham by discussing the pork he grew up eating at his grandparents' house: "Being poor, they would run out of stuff to feed their hogs along about August every year. ... They would turn their hogs loose in the forest to forage for acorns. ... It turns out that makes incredible quality pork." Having spent his childhood eating acorn fed pork, when he started in the country ham business he had problems duplicating the taste he remembered from childhood: "I tried to duplicate what they were doing, and I was using our original family recipe but my pork wasn't has good as theirs." It took him years to realize the connection between the acorn fed pigs he had enjoyed growing up and the ham he was producing, which was failing to measure up to that standard. Today, Allan relies exclusively on acorn fed hogs: "I buy from a lot of small farmers. ... They've got farmers all over [Tennessee] who are raising these old heritage breed on pasture, and I've committed to buying as many hams as they can supply me." Although he did not start curing hams professionally until 1973, it was a family tradition prior to that, and for his grandparents it was a way to feed their family. His ability to source pigs like those raised by his grandparents was a driving factor in his approach to curing hams, and he continues to develop a farm-to-table process by sourcing acorn fed pigs from local small farmers, reflecting those taste memories he hopes to share with his customers.

Recalling the livestock raised by previous generations was a driving factor for many curemasters, but for others it was not until culinary school and subsequent travel experiences that the general farming traditions they were raised with translated to pig-based products. After spending time in Italy watching and learning about raising hogs and the curing process, Jay, who was raised on a cattle farm, returned to the US and started doing some of his own research:

> The Appalachian Forest Range is the most diverse, deciduous forest range in the world, producing the most amount of food for a pig. In Europe they pride themselves on their acorns and different fed pigs. Well, here we have acorns, walnuts, hickory, paw-paws, persimmons, and all types of different fruits and nuts in order for those pigs to eat that grow naturally and in the wild across our Appalachian forest range.

Since he found a source for Appalachian-raised pigs from a farmer in West Virginia, he has been able to diversify the cured and fresh meats he produces and sells. The success he has found has placed his products on the menus of elite New York City chefs including Daniel Boulud and David Chang.

Across the "ham belt" of the South, which includes Virginia, North Carolina, Kentucky, and Tennessee, curemasters repeatedly discussed the importance of knowing what the pigs are eating, whether it is acorns in the Appalachian Mountains or peanuts in the Tidewater of Virginia. The consensus is that these details and regional variations impact the final taste of the product. Sydney explains how the flavor of pork depends on what is available for pigs to eat such as acorns or pecans, depending on what trees grow in the area:

> But that's the terroir. They're eating all these different things. So, the only real difference you're going to get in the flavor of your pigs is (a) is it free-ranging, and (b) what do you have on the ground for it to eat where you are.

He draws the comparison to terroir, or the taste of place, most commonly used in discussions of wine to describe the final products. Both wine and country ham reflect not only the skill and knowledge of the producer, but the place itself.

The changing consumer demand for local products has made it easier to sell heritage breed products, which for many is a return to family and community traditions. Rufus describes how consumer demand has impacted how his company sources pigs for their North Carolina market:

> We have cured some Ossabaw hams off the Ossabaw hog, which is from Ossabaw Island down in Georgia. We've probably cured a few more, but we started going back, people are looking for the pork and everything coming from the small farm now. And we have seen a trend with that, the biggest trend I have seen in years, you know, they want to know where everything is coming from. They want to know the farmer. They want to know the name of the farm, the type of breed; they're really wanting to know everything, their vegetables, their meats, beef, everything coming from small farms.

Although the business started out using hogs raised on local farms, over time, as the market changed in the 1980s, the company switched to large-scale farms mostly located in the Midwest. As consumer awareness increasingly resulted in a growing skepticism of industrial agriculture, however, the demand for local products changed. Now Sydney has been able to revert back to locally sourced meats with an emphasis on heritage breed pigs including the Mangalista, Berkshire, and Ossabaw. The greater consumer demand for local products taps into the producers' desire for locally raised pigs because they provide a superior final product and taste that can stand on its own in elite restaurants as well as the local family restaurant. These products are also able to compete with the traditional European imports historically dominating the market outside the South.

Country ham as a craft product

As Marcie Cohen Ferris (2014) explains, the South as a whole did not fully maintain these agricultural traditions throughout its entire history, in large part because poor sharecroppers did not have the time or resources to raise their own livestock and relied on buying cheap pork from a store. However, the 1920s and 1930s saw a concerted effort by agricultural extension agents to convince families to grow their own food. In North Carolina this program was implemented in every school and county in the state. Thus, while the emphasis on craft products is relatively new in the US and is framed in opposition to mass-produced products, across the states of the South these products and traditions never completely disappeared. For example, hog killing or pig slaughter time, the subsequent curing of meats, and using the whole animal were common long before nose-to-tail cooking was popularized by urban chefs, at a time when families raised at least a few livestock to eat throughout the year. Jay, a classically trained chef who opened a country ham business in Kentucky, summarizes these practices:

> Cook everything and preserve the entire animal so that it lasted through the summer and things as well. So, it's still a very strong practice in Kentucky and across the South to this day, it's just not seen as much. So being able to bring interpretations of some of those canning and preserving procedures back and highlight them is kind of a focus of mine, as well to kind of bring back the traditions of the rural community throughout the American South. When you look at a lot of these different dishes that they used to do, the canning of meats and whipped meats and stuff is

the same as rillettes and different types of things that are cured in Europe as well. And you can see the cultures, the culture of where it came from and how it was interpreted here before refrigeration.

Those traditions were passed down through families and became the inspiration for many to open businesses that are now run by second- or third-generation curemasters. The traditions never went away, but urbanization and migration made them less visible before the recent revitalization of interest in locally produced products.

Across the South the phrase "country ham" represents not only the product but the process of curing pork, and the distinct taste is an iconic part of Southern foodways. Outside the Southeast, however, it loses its meaning. Gregg, a professor and extension agent in the meat science department at the University of Kentucky, describes how the meaning changes outside the South:

> Here in the Southeast the country ham is the king. If you look at all the country hams that are made in this country, Kentucky, Virginia, North Carolina, and Virginia [are] where you're going to find the bulk of those being made ... along with the country bacon. Once you leave the Southeast the term "country ham" kind of loses its flair so to speak and people just know the ham as ham. Here in the Southeast you hear the term country ham and city ham. City ham is what the rest of the country knows as ham, but in the Southeast and the South there's city ham and there's country ham. ... The process to making them is entirely different. ... We jokingly call the country ham the redneck cousin to prosciutto because our forefathers from Europe brought those traditions over here and they've kind of muddled together to create this one product.

Although country ham is a traditional Southern food, the process of curing meats is not isolated or unique to the Southeast. Gregg uses the example of a country ham joke between him and his North Carolina State University counterparts to illustrate the regional specificity of country ham. Although country ham as a meaningful food is limited to the South, cured meats appear throughout the world, especially in Europe, where prosciutto and Serrano ham are common, although they are known as jamones or cured ham instead of the Southern moniker of country ham.

The success of cured ham products in the US can also be linked to the tradition and popularity of cured hams from abroad. Allan explains:

> I think maybe as people have traveled to Europe and they are better traveled and more knowledgable, I think that when they've gone to Europe and eaten the prosciutto or they've gone to Spain and eaten the Serrano they've come back here and they're thinking Hmm. Sam Edwards in Virginia or Nancy Newsom in Kentucky or Allan Benton in Madisonville, they got stuff that tastes about as good as what was found in Europe. I think they are realizing that it doesn't have to be made in Europe to be good.

While traveling abroad helped increase some people's awareness of cured meats, within the US elite chefs influenced the industry by placing country ham on their menus in place of their European counterparts (Edge, 2017).

Among these early tastemakers was James Beard, one of the first celebrity chefs in America and a driving force in the creation of modern American gastronomy (Kamp, 2006). He also shaped the country ham industry by writing about Nancy Newsom's family business. Nancy, one of the few women curemasters in the region, explains how her grandfather started the Kentucky business in 1917 where he sold country hams. Then, her father joined the business and started curing more hams.

> Then in 1963 ... he at that time took an old process and put it in a new building, he said; so he built this ham facility which is the same one I use today. ... Then in 1975 James Beard, our father of gourmet cooking, discovered our ham and began to write about it.

Despite her family's long history in the country ham business she tried to avoid becoming part of it:

> I hated this business when I was small because it took my parents away from me and they were older parents and it just pretty well depleted their energy. ... I became involved because my father was—his health was failing and I realized that my brother was nowhere around and that if something happened to him the ham business would fall on me ... so I began to learn these things on my own.

The increasing awareness and popularity of cured meats, including country ham, is also linked to the emphasis chefs place on carefully sourcing ingredients. Their popularity, coupled with family history, is responsible for many curemasters, including Nancy and Sam, remaining in the country ham business.

Although James Beard wrote about Newsom ham in the 1970s, more recently chefs have continued to highlight these local products. Allan explains how his cured hams became popular with elite chefs:

> John Fleer of Blackberry Farms told me that he loved the quality and that he wanted to develop a menu at Blackberry Farm largely around my products, and he asked me if it was okay to put my name on the menu. ... I told him it was all right, and I had no idea what in the world he was doing for me by doing that because, of course, they get incredible chefs from across the country there at Blackberry Farms and John shared my products with these people. And he single-handedly started putting my products in restaurants in other parts of the country.

The intersection of producers, chefs, and evolving consumer demands has had ripple effects throughout Southern foodways, but in many cases these small country ham producers rely on the attention garnered when elite chefs feature their products. This usage of heritage craft products, such as country ham, by elite chefs increases consumer awareness of these products' existence and how country ham can be a vibrant part of the local and slow food movements because it has always been produced in the South by small family-owned businesses.

Although country ham is the most common cured meat in the South, it is not the only one. Gregg also runs the university's butcher shop: "We cure all our own meats. We don't do a whole lot of lamb, but we've experimented with making cured lamb products. ... We do a lot of curing with our beef and pork." They rely on the university's role as a land grant institution, founded with the purpose of promoting agricultural and engineering education for the public, and the presence of large farms managed by the university for the meats sold in the butcher shop. The emphasis on research has also led Gregg and his students to experiment with curing other meats such as beef and lamb, although they have met with mixed success.

While family traditions run deep for many curemasters, others take the family tradition and apply it to new aspects of the curing process, such as going from curing bacon to curing fish. Sally, a second-generation curemaster who runs her family's trout farm, explains how she changed the business model: "The first value-added product was the caviar. ... The smoked trout was second." The chef at the farm, Charles, goes on to explain how he came to cure for the trout farm: "I don't think we had a deep curing. We did have a trout tradition. ... The curing, I was first exposed to it in culinary school." While Charles was in culinary school, he became interested in the curing traditions of the South as well as those in Scandinavia where the emphasis is on fish. The changing consumer demand for local products helped the curing industry across the South. From pork to fish, Southern curing traditions are experiencing increased popularity and consumer demand.

Lewis takes this evolution of curing meats a step further and uses one of the more popular local beverages, bourbon, as part of the curing process:

> We have a bourbon-cured that we do for both the hot and the cold smoked, and we use the Old Rip Van Winkle bourbon. We use the barrel, the staves, we run those through a chipper and the decharred material and all that goes into our hickory wood and then we also have one where we actually cure the fish in the bourbon, Old Rip Van Winkle ten-year-old bourbon.

His products receive a unique added value because the bourbon used in the curing process is one of the most highly sought after lines of bottles in the world, sometimes fetching between $500 and over $2,000 per bottle. He explains how important the younger clientele are for appreciating this food renaissance:

> Then the smoking aspect, I see the younger generation appreciating finer qualities of artisan products, and smoked fish definitely falls into the category. I see a lot more younger people, with all these wonderful food shows that are on television, they see these things and they get excited. ... So I see an opportunity there, and a lot of the young chefs are getting—that's the new things, again, is the smoked fish products.

The shift in consumer demand is not only linked to cured meats; as discussed in previous chapters, the renaissance in Southern food is not restricted to the confines of any one industry, and there is overlap between the products made and sold by a single company.

For example, although all the curemasters are known for their cured meat products, many also run small stores where they sell their hams and other products. Nancy describes some of the other products she sells at her country store in Kentucky:

> Some country items now and country foods that they used to can are now considered gourmet. Like they used to pickle okra, pickle squash, pickle green tomatoes and all like that and it wasn't a gourmet novelty, and now it is. Anything that takes time to make is gourmet food. Any food that's a natural food that takes time to make is slow food. It's in the slow food realm.

As discussed in Chapter 3, the success of the slow food movement has shifted attention to value-added products such as pickles and jams that were previously taken for granted as a part of women's labor to feed a family during the winter. Now these products are sought after by consumers as gourmet or artisanal alternatives to what can be found in supermarkets, despite their higher price points.

The success of country ham and other traditional Southern foods is part of the larger food movement, bringing consumer attention back to small family-owned businesses across the region and increasing the marketability of products previously taken for granted. Gregg explains:

> I think it's a community type thing. I think it's wanting to take care of our own and wanting to know where your food comes from, wanting to know the story behind your food, and it's really neat. It really is, because you know the local food movement has gotten huge. ... Well, classic example is when you take a vacation, you don't want to just eat at the chain restaurants. You want to eat where the locals eat. And that's kind of where this comes from.

Gregg connects the success of cured meats to the surging popularity of the local food movement across the state, and he has worked on campus to introduce local food into the dining halls.

The rise of artisanal products and the increasing number of consumers who are willing to pay more, whether at farmers' markets, elite restaurants, or small country stores that stock these products, means the producers of these artisanal ingredients are able to revive Southern traditions instead of relying on imported European ones (Edge, 2017). These products also play into the growing consumer demand for craft products as status markers within the larger foodie subculture (Johnston and Baumann, 2010). Yet, although consumers are embedding these products with new meanings that convey cultural capital to those who consume them, they are still drawing on generations of knowledge that is often overlooked in discussions of American food, especially that anchored in the South. Within the modern South these food-based traditions have been restored through community and agricultural endeavors.

Community and family

The community dynamics surrounding craft food production play out in the country ham industry in two main ways. The first is the relationship between country ham producers who work together during difficult times or share information to strengthen the industry as a whole. The second is the interaction between professional curemasters and children through the local extension programs that aim to train the next generation of curemasters who will continue the country ham tradition.

The strength of the community in the meat business becomes apparent when problems arise. In 2013, Allan's smokehouse in Tennessee caught fire and burned, but shortly after the fire he saw an outpouring of support:

> [Sam Edwards] wanted to know what he could do to help me. Could he smoke meat for me? Now that's the kind of people you got in the country ham business. ... He called and said, "This is John Ed Wompler," he said, "I've got refrigerated trucks." He said, "I've got truck drivers on standby and all the refrigeration you need." ... That's the kind of people I have been fortunate to know in the meat business. It's some of the most caring, incredible people I've ever come in contact with.

Allan is referring to the assistance that he received from the Edwards family, one of the leading Virginia curemasters, whose smokehouse burning was described in the opening discussion of this chapter. The Edwards family, like Allan, had to rely on the generosity of other producers to continue to cure their hams and keep their legacies and traditions alive until they were able to rebuild their smokehouses.

As Allan's and the Edwards family's experiences attest, when something goes wrong other curemasters step up to help, but the support offered by others goes beyond just offering resources in the wake of a fire to include educating the next generation of curemasters. Unlike most of the curemasters in this sample, Jay did not grow up learning to cure meats:

> We didn't really cure meat on the farm. Country ham is a staple for anybody in this state or area of the country. I mean, it's at every special event. So there's always been country ham around. Its primarily the focus around Christmas and Easter and Thanksgiving. ... The importance of cured meat has always been instilled in the family.

Despite not growing up knowing how to cure hams, when Jay went away to culinary school he discovered that his passion for cured meats extended far beyond the holidays. He describes how he learned the process from several established curemasters:

> [I] moved back to Kentucky working with Nancy Newsom and ... I worked a lot with Allan Benton, two of the great curemasters of North America, so working with them and understanding how they did it and their practices and their passion and what they learned from the people before them, what they've learned—so then I started curing even more meats.

While country ham was integral to the holidays when he was a child, it was not until he attended culinary school and worked with two of the leading curemasters that Jay decided to start his own business curing meats. The knowledge and techniques he learned were invaluable to his success in the industry.

It was common for the curemasters to have learned the process from their grandparents. William, the 92-year-old patriarch of his family's country ham business, explains how he got started by helping his family during hog killing time:

> My grandmother, she has an old cookbook in the house that had the recipe that the family had used for years, and one winter there she wasn't feeling too good and she pitched the book to me and said, "Here, you can do as good as I can." And that kind of started it.

In 1948, he moved from the original location, which limited him to only 100 hams at a time, to the current location and developed the business into a more commercial endeavor.

Lewis, a third generation curemaster, sums up the importance of family and tradition in driving his business:

> Family is important, and to have family in the business is important because we are all working together and we're all striving and we're all on the same page. And I feel honored that family is in the business and I feel honored that I was part of what my dad and grandfather started, so I feel good that I'm passing it on.

Although he has changed the company and diversified beyond the country hams his father and grandfather offered, the process is still the same. He explains:

> The curing and all of that, with the salmon and with the trout and things like that. That's an old-school curing technique that my dad taught me, because back in the day they used to cure bacon. So all of that salting and brining and all of that was all within our DNA. It was part of what we used to do.

Until he started curing fish, all the cured fish in the area was imported. Now the salmon is the most popular product, but the trout is almost exclusively sourced from Kentucky, and both are available on the menus of several popular Louisville restaurants.

Although not every curemaster grew up learning how to cure hams, most grew up on or near farms. Ronny describes his family history growing up on a farm:

> I was raised on a dairy farm and of course we had hogs and cattle, and there was six kids, so, you know, [my father] always killed his own hogs and we never got to eat the ham because he could sell the hams for so much more money and then buy bacon or something like that for that many kids. I guess I was grown before I eat country ham much because we just didn't get to eat it at home.

Today, Ronny and his wife Beth own one of the oldest country ham businesses in Kentucky, having bought it in 1999 when the original family who opened the business in 1909 decided to retire. Together they have learned the process of curing country ham with help from the original owner. He continues:

> The original family started the business in 1909. They actually went under [federal] inspection in 1966, and they had basically been a farm-oriented family all the years. ... Growing up in west Kentucky we had always heard of Broadbent, so it wasn't something that was new to us, and it was just something that we thought would be a good business to try.

Many families work to keep the business in the same family, but that is not an option for some; at this point, even though Ronny and Beth have grown children who help during the busiest season, it is unlikely either will continue the business.

As Ronny and Beth's experience describes, family relationships are important to the country ham industry because historically these relationships structured the industry by passing down knowledge as well as the business itself to subsequent generations, however not all subsequent generations decide to take over the family business. Ronny and Beth did not come from a country ham producing family but bought another family's business. Although not all curemasters come from traditional curing families, those who do recount their family history dating back multiple generations. Lorene, married into a country ham curing family, she explains how her late husband started curing hams in Kentucky in the 1940s: "Then my husband decided to try again, and he tried 2,000 [hams], and his father had always cured hams; it was salt cured. So he tried the sugar cured, which the hams weren't so salty. So then he has different restaurants that wanted his hams, so that's how he really started." Lorene worked at the ham house until she was 76, and today her son, Charles, Jr., runs the business. Charles, Jr. elaborates: "Our farm has been in our family since 1840, and back in the 1800s my great-great-grandmother, Susie, used to serve meat out of the family smokehouse and teas, and that's what actually started our business." Although the business started with country ham, today they are known for their ten different varieties of gourmet bacon, including a tea-flavored one in honor of Susie. "We've got some smokehouses at some of the other tenant houses, and there's one that I'm going to preserve because it's one of the original smokehouses that was done back in the 1800s. ... I mean, that's what started the whole process." The ability to draw on family history helps embed the finished products with more authenticity by connecting the consumers to the producer's personal past via a tangible product and the taste memories associated with it.

Although many curemasters are working in their family businesses, the decision process to become the next curemaster varied between families. Ron, a second generation curemaster, explains how he came to work in his family's Virginia curing business: "When you worked for my dad, you know, as soon as you were old enough to lift a ham you have to jump in there and start. ... I swore I didn't want to mess with it ever again, after I got old enough and moved away." It was not until after he was married and moved back that he took over the family business. While some, including Ron, left for a brief period of time, others never envisioned doing anything else. Rodman, a second generation curemaster who decided at a young age he wanted to be a curemaster like his father, explains the importance of the family business in Kentucky: "It's important to me to maintain the family business, to carry on, I guess you'd say. It's a way of life in the South, you know. The family is here close by; my father is still living; it's just kind of what we do, and I enjoy it." Although he was unsure if any of his three children would take over the business, they all helped out, especially during the holidays when demand is highest.

The importance of family and community extends to efforts to ensure the next generation maintains the curing traditions, through cultivated education programs such as the 4-H extension program. 4-H programs are operated in collaboration with university extension programs, focusing on youth engagement and leadership opportunities including agricultural initiatives, that aim to solve community problems. The Kentucky curemasters were the only ones who mentioned the role of 4-H extension programs in the future of country ham, through the efforts to educate children and get them involved in the curing process. Rodman explains how this program started in Kentucky:

> We have a 4-H country ham program here and as a member of the Kentucky Ham Producers, I was active in getting that started. ... We had 309 youth entered in that contest at the state fair. ... I had 43 kids that cured hams here at my plant and they came in and they do all the work. ... I'm trying to educate another generation to appreciate the products.

Beth, one of the few women curemasters, also participated in the Kentucky Ham Producers, and her family's business works with the 4-H group as well. She notes: "They auction off the 4-H ham during that opening day breakfast that we have, the 4-H students come to our plants and cure. ... We judge those hams. It was amazing this year with all those hams ... it was just amazing seeing all those kids." The children are responsible for the entire curing process, and at the end of the competition they are judged by the Kentucky Ham Producers and the winning children receive scholarship funds.

Gregg, the professor at the University of Kentucky and part of the state extension program, describes the success of the program in reaching a diverse group of children:

> We are a melting pot, and some of those old traditional lines in the sand are no longer there anymore. We do see a lot of African American kids, Asian, Hispanic, those types of kids in the projects as well. And I think 4-H has done a wonderful job of moving into the larger urban areas and convincing urban kids regardless of race or religion or whatnot that you can be involved in 4-H. ... The vast majority of our meat processors are white European [in] nature, although we do have a handful in the state that are African American, a couple that are Hispanic as well.

Gregg reiterates that the success of the 4-H program is not solely about getting children interested in curing meats, but also relates to developing a more diverse group of next-generation curemasters and creating a more inclusive country ham industry. Offering prizes for which the children compete is one way to incentivize them and to build interest and diversity in the country ham business.

The South's country ham industry is predominantly white and male. The few women curemasters in the industry are part of family businesses, and with the exception of Nancy Newsom they continue to run businesses with their husbands or other men in their family. Nancy describes the pushback she briefly received when she first took over the business, when her father's health was failing and her brother chose not to be involved in the business:

> [My father] tried to talk me out of it. When the store burned, he tried to talk me out of it. He did not want me to work that hard; and someone said, "What about your daughter running the business?" It's almost too hard for a woman; it's physically almost too hard for you. ... We lost our business in 1987, we lost the whole business. We had the hams but then we had to gain back our local people.

> The local people were what made me want to continue.
> I couldn't stand for us not to be on Main Street. We had
> been on Main Street since 1917 and I couldn't stand for
> our store not to be there.

Even though her gender led some people to question her ability to continue the family business, she was not deterred, and after the fire destroyed her family's store she used the cured hams to continue the tradition and rebuild the store. The challenges of continuing the tradition of curing meats, and of the country ham industry specifically, highlight the importance of community and family. When difficulties arise, fellow producers are able to offer resources to ensure continued production. Simultaneously, there is a need to share the knowledge and experience of curing meats with the next generation, whether within the same family or with local children through extension programs, to help ensure the strength of the industry for generations to come.

The future of country ham

Although the country ham industry is currently experiencing a culinary renaissance, along with Southern food as a whole in the US, the future of the industry is widely debated among industry insiders. On the one hand, some people argue that the culinary renaissance will ensure the success of the country ham industry for generations to come. On the other hand, others argue that country ham, although increasingly popular, is still restricted to special occasions or elite restaurants, making it too expensive to justify consuming as part of the daily repertoire of foods as it was historically.

Changes in the ham industry in general, especially the introduction of shortcuts, is seen as potentially jeopardizing the legitimacy of country ham as a whole. The importance of time in the curing process was especially stressed by the curemasters, in comparison with companies they saw taking shortcuts and producing inferior products. Rufus explains his frustration with other North Carolina ham companies: "Some ham curers ... they are able to turn the hams out in 70 to 80 days, but the country ham process is not something you can rush. ... It is a long process going through there." Although for Rufus the frustration is more general, it is also a reflection of his close proximity to the Smithfield ham company, which is a source of frustration for many in the region. As Sydney explains: "You know, they can now make a true authentic Smithfield ham in less than a month, and that's from cure all the way through age. Now, America, I ask you, is that a country ham? No. It is not. That is a warehouse ham." Sydney's frustration with the Smithfield ham company is palpable. Since the company was sold to a Chinese company and changed the processing of hams, the authenticity of the ham is questioned, particularly since they are no longer sticking to the process of curing over long periods of time to produce quality hams.

For others, among the factors to consider in deciding what to base the future of their business on are health concerns. Leslie explains why his family's curing process chooses not to use any nitrates, even though most country ham producers do: "It gives [his wife] headaches if she eats the nitrates. She will have migraine headaches. We have no additives even in our smoked sausage. We don't use the monosodium glutamate [MSG]. ... No use to using it anyhow. All it does it make it pretty in color." Although it is a family business, his wife, June, is the one in charge of the ham operation while he takes care of the cattle. Their ability to adapt the curing process to address her health concerns also makes them unique in the market, where most producers rely on additives in the curing process. Although the ability to connect to consumers' demands for healthy food, for example by avoiding the use of nitrates, is beneficial for some companies, others, including Nancy, have a less optimistic outlook on the future of the country ham industry:

> First was the issue about blood pressure and salt and then next was the issue about fat, and I don't care how many hams you try to produce, they have a better fat, you know, because the hogs are fed a different way. People are not going to want to eat "fat." They're just not going to want to eat it, and they've been taught not to eat it. I think the generation of people that understood and appreciated the ham business and that kind of thing are gone. I think it's only going to be like a specialty thing. ... It's a Kentucky nostalgia thing.

Nancy's concern that consumers don't see pork as a healthy option is only somewhat offset by the history and tradition embedded in country ham as a staple holiday food in the South, particularly in her home state of Kentucky.

Other curemasters are more optimistic about the future of country ham. Sam summarizes the evolution of Southern food he sees occurring across the US:

Southern food is riding a wave of real interest right now and country hams are a major part of that. I think we have, in true American form, they are taking country ham and crossing it with Vietnamese or Chinese or German, and it's this mixture of cultures that can take that same product from Virginia, a country ham, and use it in those dishes in a different way that people are just blown away by it. So, as long as the products are indigenous to the South historically, are being considered by these chefs, I think Southern food, at least country ham, has a good future.

Sam sees chefs as one of the main drivers in the current success of country ham. As more elite chefs seek out these craft products, the ability of the small producers to sustain their family businesses will be ensured, at least for the duration of the craft food movement.

Conclusion

The country ham industry, as with the Southern wine industry discussed in Chapter 1, has experienced a culinary renaissance. The ability to connect consumers to taste memories grounded in Southern holiday traditions and embedded in the producers' personal history of generations of curemasters is important to this renewed interested in cured meats. While the process originally relied on Mother Nature for the seasonal changes required to cure a ham, shifts in modern technology that ensure consistent temperature and humidity have helped support this heritage craft food industry. However, these new technologies have also opened the curing industry up to vulnerability from companies willing to take shortcuts using the same technology to speed up the curing process, subsequently calling into question the legitimacy of the country ham label. Yet, in the midst of the concerns about the future of the industry, the Southern foodways renaissance has brought country ham onto the menus of elite restaurants around the US and it is now seen as a legitimate alternative to its European counterparts. The ability to draw on taste memories grounded in country hams placed on holiday tables, coupled with modern consumers' desire for artisanal foods, suggests that the successful interaction between taste memory and the impression management necessary to convey the authenticity of a product has helped the industry succeed in a market historically dominated by European products and excluding those of the South such as country ham.

5

Beyond Popeye's and KFC: The Whitewashing of Southern Food Restaurants

The popular imagery of the South is often grounded in the past—large oak trees dripping in Spanish moss, the harsh and too often overlooked history of slavery, and the correspondingly large elegant plantation houses where the horrors of slavery occurred—all of which are integral parts of the origins of Southern food. Southern food calls to mind barbecue cooked over hot coals in an open pit at a roadside stand, or fried chicken and greens served on plastic tablecloths at a small family-owned restaurant. The debate over Southern foodways is often broken down into Southern/white food versus soul/black food, grounded in the historical context of racial oppression in the South. The representations of the South intertwine with racial inequality, then as now, and with food, to highlight how, for example, soul food emerged from the limited ingredients given to slaves on plantations compared with the bounty of produce and meat available to wealthy white Southerners (Miller, 2013). Inequality shaped many aspects of people's lives, including what appeared on their plates.

These representations only reflect part of the South. The South is often seen as exclusively white and black, trapped in the legacy of racial discrimination, characterized by conservative religious beliefs, and extensively rural and agrarian. However, more recently the southeastern United States has become known as the New South, with increasing appeal to tourists and those looking for a new region to call home (Stanonis, 2008). Immigration patterns have brought large numbers of blacks and whites back to the growing industry of the South as growth in other parts of the country has stagnated or declined. Although the South boasts a growing black population and increasingly cosmopolitan areas, since the early 1990s the South has also become home to a large number of Latinx immigrants, who represent over 15 percent of the population in the southern US, and a small Asian population, as well as the Indigenous groups who pre-date Europeans (Jones, 2019). This changing character of the region, while more recent and linked to large-scale immigration, also reflects the complexities of the South that have always existed, reaching far beyond the backward and racially oppressive history to reveal a complex culture filled with music, art, and food that sets it apart from the rest of the nation.

As sociologist Jennifer Jones (2019) recounts in her work on immigration patterns in the region, the South has long been home to immigrants, especially those arriving from Mexico following the manumission of slaves to serve as labor replacements for freed blacks. The South has always brought multiple racial and ethnic communities into close contact with each other, and these groups have all brought their own foodways into the region. Today, they continue to preserve their traditional foodways while simultaneously adapting to Southern foodways. For example, the dishes served at a Mexican restaurant in Kentucky reflect local ingredients, including heirloom tomatoes, duck, and beef, but the tacos are distinctly Mexican and eschew the Americanized Tex-Mex style that dominates most Mexican restaurants, with tacos smothered in sauce or cheese. This distinction can be seen in one of the most popular dishes on the restaurant's menu, short rib chilaquiles made from local beef and milled corn with a pinto-rojo sauce and topped with cotija and cilantro.

The interactions between different racial and ethnic groups around food impact the discussion of craft food, bringing traditional practices from around the world, such as handmade tortillas or kimchi, into the South. The melding of these practices with Southern foodways sheds light on how versatile craft products can be when we expand our definition. A craft product does not have to be grounded in one version of the past; it can be grounded in the past in a way that represents interactions across group boundaries, in the same way Southern food is the product of blacks and whites interacting with one another throughout history. The story of ethnic restaurants in the South compels us to look beyond the popular Southern understanding of soul or Southern food to be more inclusive of the modern South, which includes Latinx and Asian populations as well as the Indigenous groups who pre-date all other immigrant groups to the region.

This chapter explores the racial and ethnic communities across the South that are responsible for infusing the traditional understandings of Southern foodways with culturally specific ingredients and dishes. From the Lumbee Tribe in North Carolina to the Chinese grocers in Mississippi and the growing Latinx population in Kentucky, these groups have each left their mark on the food traditions of the South. However, they are often absent from discussions of traditional Southern food. One aspect of marginalization is a reliance on the invisibility of life and history to distort perceptions of who is important for cultural traditions and how they relate to structural inequalities (Ray, 2016). This chapter focuses on how these communities have navigated the balance between producing traditional foods and coping with the inequality and discrimination that continues to impact these communities today. The discussion showcases how racial and ethnic minorities are integral to Southern foodways and its history, not outliers to it.

Race and food

Southern foodways are not reducible to classical distinctions between Southern and soul food, or white and black Southerners. The modern or New South, like the country as a whole, exists in a globalized, or transnational, world, and the black–white binary long dominating racial politics in the South is now having to cope with what sociologist Eileen O'Brien (2008) calls the "racial middle." The Immigration Act of 1965 removed quotas on immigrants from Asia, Latin America, and Africa, opening the doors to immigrants in search of the mythical American Dream marked by the opportunities and consumption patterns symbolic of the American lifestyle. As the number of immigrants from around the world increased, either as voluntary immigrants seeking a better life or refugees fleeing war-torn regions, the racial demographics of the US began to change. The rates of immigration from Asia, Africa, and Latin America quickly outpaced European immigration. This, coupled with the Civil Rights movement, increasing awareness of the racial politics within the US, and the continued inflow of migrants from around the world, created distinctions that go beyond the historical white–black binary (Jones, 2019). Although there is debate over whether the "racial middle" is becoming more white or more brown (see Bonilla-Silva's [2017] *Racism Without Racists* and O'Brien's [2008] *The Racial Middle* for more in-depth discussions of these theoretical frameworks), the general agreement is that those in the "racial middle" are not afforded the same privileges as whites, and while they do not experience the same form of racism as blacks, these communities are still discriminated against (O'Brien, 2008).

Immigrants from around the world call the South home, and they have brought their foodways with them. Many of these immigrants had only their labor with which to start a new life in the US, and they began working in laundry facilities, restaurants, and as domestic servants. They cling to the idea of the American Dream and subscribe to the Protestant ethic (Weber, 2001), even when they do not use those exact words. Sue, the daughter of Vietnamese refugees, explains why she was determined to reopen her restaurant after Hurricane Katrina:

> You look at the Vietnamese people, and I look at my mother and the things that my family believes and stuff, and you look at people that can leave and flee communism to come over to America for an opportunity. And to see that they were able to leave everything they knew behind to be here in America and start a new life and able to live the American dream and to say that the storm would be something to know you out and wipe you out, I can't see that.

The opportunities afforded to those who migrated to America are seen as exceeding those available to the ones that were left behind. However, the American Dream is not without its own racial politics. Latinos' and Asians' support of the American Dream is a reflection of the framing of opportunity and social mobility as a distinctly white experience that can be obtained by some immigrants, but not all, and black community members continue to be denied opportunities for stability, let alone advancement (Portes and Zhou, 1992; Portes and Zhou, 1993; Yancey, 2003; Treitler, 2013).

Monica, a Chinese immigrant, explains how hard work accounts for her success in business:

> Everything we learn by ourselves because we're from a different world, from Hong Kong; we sit in the office, yeah, from here; you have to work long hours, but one thing we keep in mind, and talk to ourselves, because this is our business, so we learn by our own talent and with dedication.

Monica relates her experiences since moving to the US 25 years ago, when she and her husband started a grocery store. Although she does not mention the Protestant ethic, her description of hard work, talent, and individual success without outside assistance echoes the definition of the Protestant ethic. The hard work linked to the restaurant industry, in general, is presented as a recurring element in the restaurant owner's passion and drive. Izmene explains why she decided to open a restaurant:

> The passion is mainly the work in general. It's not just having a source of income but really the love for work. I've always been independent. I've always dedicated myself to work. I've never been a housewife. ... I get up every day making breakfast, making meals, and do them with all the love possible that I can put in this food.

When she and her husband moved to Kentucky because his job transferred him from the Mexico-based office to the US headquarters, she decided to focus on her passion: cooking.

The passion for cooking underlies many of these restaurant owners' decisions to participate in the industry. Francisco, whose brothers had opened several restaurants, joined them in the business after he moved to Kentucky. Even though he started as a dishwasher, he enjoys the work: "Everything that is work I like, I love. I love the work, it's something sacred." He describes what he has gained from working: "One starts learning a lot of communication. I've taken all of this as a school because everything that I've learned in English, I have learned here in the restaurant." While the subscription to the Protestant ethic underlies how many restaurant owners talk about their passion for work, the restaurant industry was also repeatedly referred to as a place of learning, especially for immigrants who are learning to speak English.

Despite their hard work and subscription to the American Dream rhetoric, some feel they are seen not as entrepreneurs but as competition by their white counterparts:

> There are many entrepreneurs and many are Latino. ... I hope that in two years the Anglo-Saxon market will recognize us as Latino entrepreneurs, because we are trying to change the economy, we are not here standing in the way, we are contributing, we pay our taxes, that we are growing the community. All businesses are giving work, even to the Anglo-Saxons.

Montzerat describes the changes she has seen in the local community as more Latinx open small businesses and what she sees as the origins of this increase in business:

> I think that Latinos always come to this country with the desire to get ahead, to push ahead, to success, to have your own house, to have your own car, all that. I think we all come with that dream. ... It's like that immigrant brotherhood. I hope they do well, that everything works.

Even though the increasing number of businesses means additional competition, she does not look at this as a negative situation. Instead, she sees it as a positive development that more Latinx are opening businesses and working toward the "dream," as she calls it.

As historian Yong Chen (2014) explains regarding the history of Chinese food in the US, regardless of how successful Chinese grocery stores and restaurants are economically, their location reflects the national politics of the era when they were founded, especially those that opened prior to the Civil Rights era. Chinese restaurants and grocery stores were originally located in African American neighborhoods or Chinatowns. Historically, the food of Chinese immigrants was marginalized and degraded by white consumers as dirty or containing rats and dogs as sources of meat. This reflects the broader marginalization and discrimination of Chinese immigrants in the US: they were seen as less than white, but in most areas they were still ranked above blacks socially, placing them in the "racial middle" (O'Brien, 2008). Raymond, the son of Chinese immigrants, describes his childhood growing up working in his father's grocery store: "My mother did the cooking, but everybody worked in the grocery store. I just know that when we were able to start counting, we worked." His father's grocery store was located in an African American neighborhood, but the store attracted a diverse clientele. He explains the overlap between his mother's cooking and that of his peers' mothers: "Mother would have to skin the chicken, but it was very fresh. ... It's called bak jamgai, but basically what it was is just steamed chicken. But I didn't realize that most [of] the Caucasian people and African American only had fried chicken." It was not until he was in fifth grade that he realized his family's foodways were different than those of his classmates.

The American understanding of ethnic foodways historically blended the regional food of an entire country together into one conceptualization of that cuisine. For example, although Chinese food has regional differences rooted in place-based cuisines such as Cantonese and Sichuan, those differences are often ignored within the US context. Sichuan is a province in western China known for its spicy and distinctive dishes. China can be divided into four or five regional cooking styles, but it was not until the 1960s that these distinctions came to be known within the US ethnic food context (Chen, 2014). The regional specificity is becoming an increasingly common motivator for restaurant chefs who want to serve authentic regional foodways and a clientele seeking out these experiences as authentic and exotic (Johnston and Baumann, 2010). Heng and her husband, Cori, were both born in China and now own a Sichuan Chinese restaurant in Houston. She says their goal is to introduce authentic Chinese food to Houston: "Basically to introduce the real authentic Chinese—well, Sichuan—cuisine to American people. ... Our American people friends, all they know about Chinese food is orange chicken, Kung Pao chicken, some kind of fried rice, everything you can find from Panda Express." Americans' knowledge of ethnic foodways is often shaped by fast food, such as Panda Express, or the local variations of ethnic cuisine such as Tex-Mex dishes instead of the regionally specific dishes that appeal to a Mexican clientele or those willing to try the cuisine (Pilcher, 2012).

Fabian explains how he is updating the menu for the restaurant his father started in 1989: "That's one of the things that me and my dad are doing now, is trying to change the menu to really reflect Mexican cooking, because what we had before was more Tex-Mex. I mean, of course it was Mexican but not your traditional, like, sopes or gorditas or torta or pozole." The decision to serve authentic Mexican food has led many chefs to abandon Tex-Mex in favor of regionally specific Mexican dishes. Francisco describes the menu changes he has made to the restaurant: "I take care of my style, my meals. People say it is the most original, the most authentic Mexican. For me that's an honor. ... I changed the recipes. I gave it better flavor to food. More or less, a little of what is really Mexican food." Although the Tex-Mex style of Mexican food, smothered in cheese and sour cream, dominated the food scene when he first opened his restaurant, he is altering the menu to reflect what he labels authentic Mexican cuisine, which is grounded in his taste memories from childhood.

These menus and alterations are continually shaped by an increasing awareness of what Mexican food looks like in Mexico. Laura explains how the menu at her restaurant evolved with each trip she made back to Mexico to gather recipes and knowledge from friends and family members, which she and her husband then used to shape the dishes on the menu:

> We had a good response from people with Mexican food, with the authentic stuff. The beef head, the tongue, which many people haven't tasted. But you'd be surprised how many Americans like to eat this food as well, because they don't come for the burrito, no! They come for authentic. They say, "Give it to me the way you eat it."

Chefs' decisions to focus on authentic regional foodways also impact their clientele, who are increasingly seeking out these restaurants for their grounding in specific foodways traditions.

According to historian Jeffery Pilcher (2012), it was not until the 1980s that Mexican food, not the Tex-Mex version of the southwestern US, came to be popular across the United States. Subsequently the popularity extended far beyond the fast food chains and boxed taco mixes to include upscale Mexican restaurants across the country as well as the increasingly common taco truck that together have reshaped the image of Mexican food to reflect the regional variations across the country. These differences play out in what dishes a restaurant serves as well as the clientele who seek out those dishes.

Embedded in discussions of traditional ethnic foodways is a respect for tradition and innovation, which can be described as an art form. Arun describes his experience with the cuisine of Punjab, a region in northern India: "Now I'm creating my own—cooking for me, it's like art. I love to play with the spices. ... A lot of fusion dishes. There's a lot of trend right now, like Indian–Chinese dishes are really popular, especially in [the] Indian community." Arun started helping in his uncle's California-based restaurant when he immigrated to the US from Punjab 25 years ago. Today, he owns his own Indian restaurant in Arkansas, across the street from a Tyson chicken plant that employs over 500 people, about 40 percent of whom are Indian. He explains that despite the location of his restaurant, there is still variation in the clientele:

> North Indian people do not go out and eat in North Indian restaurants, because they believe that the women and ladies can cook better than the restaurant. ... South Indians are the one, they'll come in here and they're regular customers here on the weekend. Because their food is a little bit different than mine.

Among the South Indians who frequent his restaurant, the most popular dishes are the breads (naan, tandoor, and paratha), commonly found in North Indian cuisine but less commonly in the rice-based cuisine of South India. Yet these variations are foundational to the sense of art that makes each chef's food distinct and to the ability to preserve the knowledge of this cuisine.

Other restaurants offer a blend of dishes from various regions. Abhijeet describes the variety of Indian food his restaurant serves: "We just took some of the best of what we liked within India, within all the states of India. So, you have eastern and western and northern and southern food." His wife, Lisa, continues: "We compete with individual Indians' memories of what their home kitchen was, because we're making dishes every family made at home, but they made it a little differently, because their mothers customized the spice blends." There are slight variations to these familiar dishes, especially when it comes to the blends of spices. Developing the spice blend for these ethnic restaurants to connect to the taste memories of their home kitchens historically has been difficult throughout the South (Abarca, 2017). Although there were large-scale distributors and ethnic grocery stores in the US, these were often located on the West Coast or in major urban areas such as Houston and Chicago, making it a challenge for family-owned restaurants outside these locations to source the necessary ingredients to complete their dishes. Although sourcing specific spices and ingredients is difficult for ethnic restaurants across the South, Arun explains that there are similarities between Indian and other cuisines: "Mexican is too close to Indian. ... They do more corn and less white [flour]. We do white [flour] and wheat, less corn. ... Main spices they use is the main spices we use. And vegetables of course. Tomatoes, onions, jalapenos, these are the main three things, and cilantro." The similarities between the two cuisines make it possible for Indian restaurant owners such as Arun to source spices from Mexican grocery stores, which are more accessible in the region than Indian grocers.

For others, the solution was to open a store that provided the necessary ingredients to members of the local community. Ali describes the connection between his religion and his decision to open his own meat market:

> We are Muslim, we have to have halal meat, cannot get any kind of meat. And we had to drive all the way to Dallas or Tulsa or Kansas City to pick up fresh meat, so that's why we came up with the idea to just open my own shop and serve

the community here and make sure it's halal 100 percent
and its fresh meat.

Even though his decision was motivated by his religious background,
the Arab community in the area is very small and a majority of his
customers are not Muslim; many of them are from India or other
cultures who appreciate the availability of fresh, never frozen, meat.
The ability to access the necessary spices or meat needed to complete
a dish allows the consumer to be transported to the past by taste
memories (Abarca, 2017).

Culinary memories are often grounded in childhood experiences.
Izmene discusses the importance of culinary traditions to her family
when she was a child in Guadalajara:

> Life in Mexico takes place day by day in the kitchen.
> Everyone who had the good fortune to grow up in Mexico
> know that it's there where the family converges. Since
> childhood I also was fortunate to be born into a family
> that has a great passion for food. ... I saved my memories
> of smells from a young age—the smell of chile, the smell
> of chocolate. Fresh food every day. Fresh tortillas. I have
> them [as a] memory, and I continue sharing them here
> in America.

This, combined with her husband's passion for food, led them to open
a breakfast restaurant. He explains: "Most restaurants you'll find here
open at noon. ... They offer what Americans usually know about
Mexican food, but few have heard of Mexican breakfast, which is what
the Mexican wake up to every day at Grandma's house, at Mom's house,
and begins his day." The ability to recreate those taste memories, even
thousands of miles away, helps drive the dishes that appear on these
menus. It also introduces consumers to less well-known versions of
food from around the world.

The ability to connect people to another place, especially their
country of origin, is a driving force for many restaurant owners.
Montzerat explains how the Mexican dishes she misses have influenced
what appears on her menu: "We craved the esquite like in Mexico
City, it is prepared with onions and epazote and all of that, and
here we didn't have that. So we started making it more for our own
craving and we discovered other people were craving the same thing."
Her husband continues: "First it was the sorbet, and people loved
it because they hadn't had one like the ones in Mexico. You taste

one of the sorbets, and it takes you straight—it doesn't matter where you are from in Mexico—it takes you back to whatever place where you tried a sorbet like that." The combination of dishes and flavors unique to Mexico plays into the distinct memories people have of home: "People need to remember where they came from, and flavors are a way to do it. I have found myself in that situation where I say, 'I am going to eat an esquite to remember.' ... That's something all immigrants have, that need to remember." Similarly, Sayed describes how popular the bread-based dishes in his restaurant are among the South Indian community in the area: "Our puri, they say, is just like their home, their mom used to make. The chefs' cooking is a little bit different than women cooking at home, so if somebody like his mother's recipes, then he likes our recipes." The connection between homestyle cooking and the food at his restaurant continually draws customers seeking that feeling of home.

A large portion of the clientele at many of these restaurants and grocery stores, at least originally, were fellow immigrants, but an establishment's location could help expand its customer base. Frieda explains how her family's grocery store attracted a diverse clientele: "Our store had a premium meat market and that would draw in the white customers, who would want certain roasts or steaks. The black customers probably wanted things, I guess we would call it soul food, like ham hock and salt meat." Although she is describing stereotypical representations of Southern verses soul food regarding the cuts of meat people selected, the store was able to attract customers from across social groups. Noi explains that the diverse clientele that frequents her family market appears to reflect the larger Houston ethos: "It's so many cultures that I think it's happening here in Houston, and that's why we see those people at least coming here, that I can see they are coming from different places and they are willing to try new things and learn a different culture, at least on the food." The desire to learn about a variety of ethnic foodways was a recurring theme across these restaurants and grocery stores.

The ability to draw on taste memories of distant places, spaces, and time allows restaurant owners to highlight the uniqueness of their food for their customers, who then identify their restaurants as "authentic" eateries that they continually support. Surekha explains how the chapati, an Indian flatbread, became popular in the local community:

> Indians obviously [know] because it's their staple diet. But for Americans they didn't know. We had to introduce it to them and explain it to them, so we had to come up with

some sort of comparison. That's why we used the word tortilla because they were more used to Mexican food.

The success of the chapati in her restaurant was dependent on being able to compare it to the more well-known tortilla. Once the awareness of a dish or cuisine increases in the community, the clientele stop reflecting the ethnicity of the food and instead become more representative of the larger community. Rosa explains how popular her gorditas are outside the Latino community: "I get a lot of American too. Blacks. They all come and everybody likes food. They say they are the best gordita they have tasted. It is the best food."

Generally speaking, ethnic restaurants serve two key purposes aside from the utilitarian economic and profit margins of any business. First, they create the opportunity to access taste memories for immigrants in a new land (Garcia, DuPuis, and Mitchell, 2017). Second, they increase consumer awareness of regional cuisines for anyone willing to eat at the restaurant (Johnston and Baumann, 2010; Pilcher, 2012). Ethnic food is becoming increasingly popular in the US. Chinese restaurants have become the most widespread cuisine in the nation, topping the number of popular fast food restaurants, specifically Burger King, KFC, and McDonald's combined (Chen, 2014). Subsequently, as a subculture of foodies arises, ethnic restaurants, as long as the food they serve is seen by consumers as authentic to that ethnicity, come to represent exotic experiences that convey social capital to the consumer (Johnston and Baumann, 2010).

Blended foodways

All the restaurant and store owners are known for their ethnic food, but although they all serve these regionally specific dishes to others, their home kitchens tell related stories of immigration and acculturation through the incorporation of distinctly American foods, often at the cost of their country-of-origin foods (Garcia, DuPuis, and Mitchell, 2017). Traditional ethnic foodways and regional Southern foodways often merge over time as immigrants adjust to American cultural norms, or children ask for the American-style meals they see their classmates eating. Joe explains how the language barrier he experienced growing up impacted family mealtime:

> [Mother] would only speak Chinese, and growing up we only spoke English, so we had to ask our dad. Say, "Well, Daddy, tell Mama to cook us some fried chicken and pork

chop." He would say, "Son, if you want your mother to cook your pork chops or fried chicken, you've got to start learning how to speak Chinese."

Even as a child, Joe and his sibling wanted their mother to prepare more Americanized foods such as fried chicken instead of the traditional Chinese dishes she was familiar with cooking. He explains that even as his mother learned to cook American foods, dinner time was still problematic, because "[my father] liked fried chicken and fried pork chops but he always had to have his Chinese [dishes], rice and some vegetables. He always had to have that because if he didn't, he'd always say there is nothing here for me to eat." This forced Joe's mother to balance her children's desire for American food with her husband's demand for traditional Chinese dishes. The result was often something fried, such as chicken or pork, to satisfy the children and side dishes of rice and Chinese vegetables to satisfy her husband. Dishes such as macaroni and cheese and spaghetti were not cooked because the bok choy and rice would not fit with the rest of the meal.

The desire to fit in with one's classmates was an important driver for families such as Joe's to Americanize their diets, but in other cases it became a point of resistance and a way to embrace the ethnic cuisine of their country of origin (Gabaccia, 2009). Cori explains how difficult it was for him to adjust to American food as a child: "I didn't like the food that's offered in the school. I found myself starving the whole time because I didn't like cheese, and I didn't like fried chicken and all that stuff. ... So I found myself bringing my own food to school, Chinese food, and eating with chopsticks." While his classmates found his eating habits strange and different, for him it marked one of the more difficult points of assimilating to American culture.

Other families found a balance between their traditional country-of-origin dishes and the regional cuisine of their new home. Araceli explains that she cooks the traditional Mexican dishes she grew up eating but has made an effort to learn about Southern food, which she also enjoys: "I think Cracker Barrel has the most traditional Kentucky food, and I love going to Cracker Barrel. I really like the biscuits and how they prepare the fish. Although Kentucky does not have much ocean, but rivers, the river fish tastes very good. I have not prepared Kentucky food here yet." Even though she only goes out to eat for Southern food, instead of cooking it at home or in her own restaurant, she enjoys the experience. Her business partner, Sandra, continues: "What I see, if that Kentucky food is fried meat, chicken, even pork, all that is like food in Romania, my country." Sandra explains that although she is new to the South, she sees a lot of similarities between Southern foodways and Romanian cuisine.

The bridge between local and country-of-origin foodways is a recurring theme for many ethnic restaurants across the South. Sue explains how she uses food to bridge cultural differences in her local community:

> A Vietnamese Po'boy that we do, which is kind of a Po' Boy as in the Southern side of the sandwiches. But the Vietnamese side of it would be all of our different types of meats and marinades and even the vegetables that we put on the sandwich. ... It's almost a hybrid between the two.

Sue's Mississippi restaurant works to bridge the gap between Southern food and the familiar Vietnamese foods that members of the community grew up eating. Not all the restaurants had such hybrid dishes, however, and the balance was most frequently discussed in regard to home cooking.

For other families the holidays, especially Thanksgiving, became a merging point for traditional ethnic cuisine. Thanksgiving is a uniquely American holiday, complete with its own distinct food culture and traditions that date back to the 1800s (Smith, 2003). Frieda recalls her mother's experience learning about American food culture as a young wife and recent immigrant at age 18:

> For Thanksgiving and Christmas, we would always have turkey and dressing but you could also have chow mein. ... There were other Chinese moms and I guess they exchanged recipes and such. But she definitely incorporated the American with the turkey. Then Easter we had ham, and July Fourth barbecue. I think because my mother was younger, she was more eager to learn about American food culture.

For Frieda's mother, it was not only her desire to consume the parts of American culture that are seen as traditional holidays with established foodways, such as turkey on Thanksgiving, ham on Easter, and barbecue on the Fourth of July, but it was also a source of community as these young immigrant wives shared their growing knowledge of the cultural foodways of their new home.

The shared knowledge of American recipes, and the ability to learn new dishes, was a starting point for many immigrant families. Monica explains how she learned to cook American food after moving to the US as a young adult from China and having a difficult time sourcing the familiar Chinese ingredients:

> I started learning here. I start letting my customers look at the recipe, look at the cookbook, and look at the Food Channel and try to cook American food. ... I try to learn a lot of American food because me and my husband, the goal to come here and just try to go in the America. Whatever you take your life to go somewhere, you need to be pleased over there. So we try to learn everything we could; tried to adjust to life in America. ... I still cook Chinese food. ... We just buy some soy sauce, oyster sauce, chili sauce and stuff, but it cannot compare to Hong Kong.

Even though she still cooks Chinese food, sourcing the ingredients is difficult and often involves a trip to Memphis, over an hour's drive away. She explains that despite the difficulty in sourcing ingredients, she still tries to recreate the dishes she grew up eating in China.

Sourcing authentic ingredients, whether for cooking at home or in the restaurant, was a recurring problem, particularly in the 1970s and 1980s. The solution varied among families but often involved growing the produce in their backyards or making a trip of more than 100 miles to a large metro area such as Chicago or Houston, as Raymond explains: "Now initially I remember we didn't have stuff like bok choy and things like that. That normally came out of San Francisco or Chicago. Now you can order it from a lot of different places. But at that time there were none." Raymond recalls how difficult it was to source Chinese ingredients when his father opened the restaurant in the 1970s. However, as the cuisine became more popular throughout the US, the commercial market expanded to include at least some traditional ingredients (Pilcher, 2012; Chen, 2014).

The lack of ingredients forced some chefs to become increasingly creative with their dishes, to merge the tastes of their country of origin with the available American produce. Sreepathy describes her problem finding Indian vegetables in Arkansas:

> When I was living in Houston, even the Indian vegetables were available in Walmart. I never felt that I was not in India. But when I came here, that's when I realized it's not. You have to adapt. I would not eat most of the vegetables that were available in Walmart. The American section, like

celery, unh-uh. Then I learned how to make curry with
it, because that's what's available here.

The limited access to Indian vegetables forced her to merge Indian
cuisine with American ingredients to create the unique taste her
restaurant is known for today. Laura remembers that when her family
moved to Kentucky, it was difficult to find Mexican ingredients without
making the over five-hour drive north to Chicago. Today, she is able to
source local ingredients for her restaurant and tortilleria: "We buy the
maize locally. The company is called Weisenberger Mills. ... Every week
we buy 12 sacks. ... Then you cook it. And we make tortilla daily." The
resurgence of heritage grains in the South has also solved some of the
problem of sourcing ingredients for many restaurants, who are able to
partner with local farmers to grow produce to meet their specific needs.

For others the solution was to open an ethnic grocery store in
the region to meet their family's needs as well as the needs of other
immigrant families in the area. Noi explains the sourcing problems her
family's Asian market solved: "Noodle, curried paste, coconut milk,
all day. And right now, Americans are, whoever wants to cook Thai
food can come here." Her husband, Lawrence, continues: "They come
in with their cookbooks. After going to Thailand and taking a class
or just interest and having never been there but still have an interest
in Thai cooking." Even though their store is small, they are able to
provide a majority of the necessary ingredients to customers who are
interested in Thai cuisine. He explains that they source some of those
products from local farmers: "The little community down there, mainly
Cambodians, there's some Laos there, but they've been there for a
while and they grow the morning glory [greens]. The summertime
is really an abundance of vegetables." Noi continues: "Some unique
vegetables that normally you can't find anywhere. ... They just grow
it and then they bring it to us. We're the only one who is selling that
for Thai or Laos communities."

These families made long trips or opened their own grocery stores
to resolve issues with sourcing ingredients to support the dishes of their
traditional ethnic foodways. Simultaneously, immigrant families to the
South absorbed the cultural variations of both the region and their new
nation to craft a unique blended culture around food. This blended
approach reflects the important diversity in Southern foodways that is
overlooked by many people who fall back on stereotypes about who
lives in the South and what they eat. However, despite these families
describing their many successes in adjusting to life in America, and
the South in particular, they have also faced discrimination.

Discrimination

Sociologist Eileen O'Brien (2008) describes how those in the "racial middle" experience discrimination, but there is a qualitative difference between their experiences and the experiences of black families in their communities. Although Asian and Latino immigrants experience prejudice, stereotypes, exclusion, and marginalization overall, they often minimize the impact and frequency of discrimination in their lives. Accounts of immigrant experiences surrounding food are filled with discrimination, especially when a new cuisine first arrives in an area. For example, there are many harsh stereotypes of questionable meats and unhygienic sanitary practices that plague Mexican and Chinese restaurants despite their growing popularity (Pilcher, 2012; Chen, 2014). Luck describes the 50 years of success that his family's grocery store enjoyed in the context of race in the Mississippi Delta:

> We didn't feel the discrimination that a lot of Chinese in the Delta has. We were sort of fortunate because we were the only Chinese family there. And if you notice, if you're a minority, as long as you are still a minority, say one family, you don't have any trouble or anything. But when the two or three families move in, you know, the other people begin to get a little jittery. ... But being the only Chinese family, we experienced very little prejudice. Of course, we had it. I'm not trying to fool myself.

Although the Mississippi Delta is known for its contentious race relations, especially between whites and blacks throughout the Jim Crow and Civil Rights eras, Luck's family restaurant remained open throughout that time period. While he acknowledges the existence of prejudice, he remembers very little of it when they were one of the only Chinese families in the area.

Although the racial politics in the South would not appear to attract immigrants looking for a better life for their families, the region was seen as offering a safer home and a closer-knit community than was available elsewhere. Francisco explains his decision to leave California and relocate to Kentucky: "There was a good amount of Latinos. A lot of Latino business, but not as many as today. It was a city that's too big, with many conflicts, many gangs. I did not feel comfortable in that city." He relocated to Kentucky in 1999 and started working in the restaurant industry before opening his own restaurant. The Latinx community has evolved in the region, beginning with many changes in the late 1980s and into the 1990s. Laura describes how the Latinx community has evolved in Kentucky since her family moved to the area in the mid-1980s:

> At first, they were just get-togethers to make friends. Then the birthdays ... Christmas. We also started celebrating Thanksgiving. Later on, were the quinceaneras. ... There were 40 of us; we'd go all the way to Springfield to hear a Mass in Spanish. ... It was a beautiful thing because in those days, we all got together and there was no rancor.

Today, there is a larger population of Latinx people in the region, and the close-knit friendships Laura recalls are not as common.

Although the South provides immigrants with a sense of community, it is not without problems. Francisco describes his experiences with discrimination since moving to Kentucky:

> I believe that in this city there isn't too much discrimination, there isn't too much racism against Latinos. ... Out of nowhere you do feel it sometimes in a business, some place where you go that are American businesses. Sometimes they see you as a nothing. Many times, they don't even bother to take notice of you. But unfortunately, that's what one has to face being in a country that's not yours.

Francisco acknowledges that being an immigrant in the country comes with discrimination and racism. Fabian describes the changes he has seen in the level of acceptance of Latinx people by the local community:

> I mean, we're in the South, so racism has always been here. When we first came here, I know that they used to turn their backs on us. ... We're more accepted. It's really changed throughout the years. You see more and more hispanos. ... I don't think they can turn their backs on us anymore.

The Latinx population is quickly growing in the US, and although both Francisco and Fabian recount how it was easier for Southerners, particularly whites, to be racist in the past, the large numbers of Latinx in the region have made it more difficult in many ways. This experience of acceptance as the population increases contrasts with Luck's experience, in which racism worsened as more Chinese immigrants moved into the area. These changes in the perception of immigrants and subsequent political and social support or punitive response are not uncommon as the size of the immigrant population grows and economic growth stagnates (Jones, 2019).

Unlike the Chinese and Latinx immigrants in the South, with their relatively recent histories, the Lumbee are one of the original Indigenous communities whose presence in the area pre-dates the arrival of Europeans. Heaverd describes his experience as a member of the Lumbee Tribe growing up in the segregated South:

> In the 1930s, 40s, 50s, and 60s we had three races of folks here. So, I grew up as an Indian, and my opinion, I didn't have the same privileges as my white friends. For example, we had a theater—the whites went downstairs, the blacks and Indians went upstairs. But I always had a feeling that I was just as good as anybody else.

He remembers growing up watching Indigenous soldiers return from war: "We lost a lot of them in the War and when—went off to fight for our country and they were denied going to a theater with everybody else. They were denied going to a restaurant where it had white only." He describes his experiences with discrimination: "We were known as the Cherokees and also the Croatans and then were known as the Lumbees, but that's our name today. ... We wanted the name Lumbee because we settled down from the Lumber River." Although the Lumbee people succeeded in being recognized by the federal government as a tribe in 1956 and later received additional recognition in 2009, the problems continued: "We want to be federally recognized. We are federally recognized with name only." Federal recognition comes with a series of benefits, including tribal sovereignty, for Indigenous groups, but the Lumbee are still not a fully federally recognized tribe. Although he does not use the word racism or discrimination, the very identity of being a member of the Lumbee, or another Indigenous group, comes with sharp politics intertwined with federal policy. The Lumbee continue to fight for the privileges associated with being a federally recognized tribe today.

Family-owned restaurants

Large cities such as Nashville, Atlanta, and Charlotte are becoming Southern cosmopolitan meccas for the young educated middle class seeking out white-collar industries, art, and the subsequent gentrification that goes along with them. The population of the South is growing, due to both an influx of immigrants and the return of whites and blacks whose ancestors left the South. Many of these cities are also home to growing refugee populations. These demographic changes in Southern communities, coupled with industrial and economic changes, can impact families' lives. Economic loss is a problem for many small towns across the region, particularly for families who own restaurants and rely on local residents as their main customer base. These changes continue to shape the experiences of small family-owned restaurants and grocery stores. Joe explains how the clientele at his family's Arkansas restaurant has changed since it opened in the 1960s: "The hospitals are the big industry now but back then it was just people were working for big farms. If you're not in the grocery business like that, you know, there's no other industry or business back then." Because of the farming community, his dad would open the restaurant at 4 am and stay open until midnight to serve the people coming and going from the farms. As the farms closed, he shortened the restaurant's hours.

Callie explains how deindustrialization has impacted her North Carolina restaurant:

> I opened up, I think it was April 8, 1987, and it was like heaven. It was busy. I was really, really busy, always was busy, especially when the plants was around here. See, most of the plants are gone now and people goes now to the fast food places unless they want homecooked meals and they come here.

Although the home cooking her restaurant is known for continues to draw in customers, the disappearance of a large number of jobs linked to the loss of local industry makes it more challenging to continue to operate a small business. The ability to offer customers an alternative to fast food chains is important, but the economics are still difficult: "It offers an opportunity for something that's not a chain. Family-owned restaurants are hard in small towns because the economics of them are just hard." Although Lisa and Abhijeet's restaurant is important to the community, the difficulty of running a small business permeates their decision-making process.

Family-owned businesses have to cope with deindustrialization as well as increased competition. Frieda explains how consumption patterns have changed in her family's Mississippi grocery store: "The shopping pattern has changed. People aren't coming in there buying a week's worth of groceries like they were when I was growing up. Now they are coming in for convenience things." Local stores are no longer the only option when shopping for groceries. Monica describes the challenges her business is facing as the economy of the South evolves: "We have a lot of long-time customers, they're very loyal. ... The new customer, they need to adjust to it because we're an independent store. The price is a little bit high and cannot compete with the big Giant. ... We try to do our best to provide the community." Unlike their chain counterparts, family-owned businesses are grounded in the local community, but they also have to cope with the social situation around them, which in the South includes a complex history surrounding race and class.

Monica explains why she thinks the number of small Chinese-owned stores has decreased:

> The first one, that nobody take over. The second one is the large supermarket, but the neighborhood, I don't know. I think it's just like us to raise the next generation, when they get a job, they all move, and they take their parents out of here. So, I think it's nobody to take over, and then besides the competition of the giants, like Walmart, Kroger, so the children don't want the parents to work hard like that.

Her husband, Tony, continues: "I think the small store will disappear. Most of the chain stores will take over. Mainly I stay so long in this kind of store because I am waiting for the next generation to grow up." Although their store remains open, neither is optimistic about the store's future because the competition from large corporations is a deterrent to the next generation taking over.

Family-owned businesses in the South have to navigate the racial politics of the region along with deindustrialization, which is impacting the economic stability of many small towns across the South. Several of these family-owned restaurants have operated for multiple generations and coped with the ever-changing South. Raymond's father made the decision to close his Mississippi-based grocery store and leave the state after someone threw a brick through the glass window of his store during the race riots of the Civil Rights movement in the Deep South, causing him to question the safety of the area. He moved the family to South Carolina and opened a restaurant when Raymond was in tenth grade: "He finally decided to do that 'cause at that time there were only a few Chinese restaurants in the South. ... So by the time he finally opened it was pretty much an overnight success."

Other families who have recently opened restaurants hope their establishments can operate as a cultural bridge for their communities.

Lisa explains her vision for community building at her family's Indian restaurant:

> My brother, who looks like a big redneck, and he was in a truck and he drove up and there was a group of Muslim women praying in our parking lot. So, he was happy to see them and got out to say hello, but he scared them, because you can imagine in [Arkansas], if you're praying on a prayer rug and some redneck comes up to you, you're not really sure of the response. He managed to convey to them, "Hey, I'm friendly, I'm glad you are here," but that's the type of experience we've loved. We want to facilitate that sense of, here at the table we can all sit together and have a meal, and all be a part of the larger family.

For Lisa and her husband, the ability to act as a bridge with the local Indian and Muslim community is an important goal of their restaurant, which reflects their interracial marriage.

Foodways not only serve as a bridge to community members across class and racial divides, but they are also a resource for the next generation to access more opportunities, especially through church fundraisers:

> For 25 years I was the fundraiser for the youth department and we would sell yock and we would take the kids away for a whole week and, you know, for us to raise $20,000 and $25,000 so the kids would not have to pay, because a lot of times the parents don't have the money to take their kids on a vacation. So our church was very instrumental on making sure the kids got out for entertainment, educational, religious, whatever. ... They'd go to black universities and some of our kids has graduated from Bethune Cookman, A&T, because we took them.

Mary describes the profitability of selling yock, a noodle-based dish with roots in both Chinese and African American foodways, in the community to fund the church youth group's activities and ensure children could participate regardless of their parents' ability to pay. Providing children with more opportunities or a safe place to gather was frequently mentioned as a goal of restaurants across the South. Although Montzerat's business morphed into a restaurant, it began as a community gathering place for members of the local Latinx community:

> When we started our project [it] was to connect with the community and become a local house of culture where the kids can spend time. … Connecting with the kids, who come, who feel safe, that the parents feel confident that they are here. That we are not trying to hurt them, that nothing is going to happen here.

Parents in the community began to see the business as a safe place for their children to spend time after school, protected from the rising crime and drug problems in the community.

The desire to create opportunities for children also extends to parents' desires for them to either enter into the business or seek out alternatives to the restaurant industry. Luck explains that his father pushed his children to go to college and succeed in new ways: "My dad pushed the education. He really didn't want any of us to be in the grocery business, but it was easy. That's sort of the easy way out. And he made up my mind that I was going to college." Although Luck's brothers ended up in the grocery store business, Luck was one of the first Chinese men to graduate from the University of Mississippi, in 1950. Luck's family continues to succeed in the grocery business, but going to college was a requirement, with the business as a backup.

Although some parents are opposed to their children taking over the family business, others hope they will do so. Jacklyn explains why she hopes her son will take over the family restaurant, which has been open for 25 years: "Hopefully to keep the tradition. My dad worked really hard for this restaurant, and we want to keep it in our family." The ability to keep a business in the same family for multiple generations serves as a powerful motivator for the entire family, not only the next generation. Emma explains how she came to run her family's fish market after her uncles stepped down:

> He became sick and had to take him away from the business. Then my other uncle had to step up and take it. It was taking him away from his ministry, doing what God wanted him to do. He was getting ready to close the business. I decided to come take over to keep it in the family.

Although she is currently running the business, she hopes to pass it down to the next generation: "I love my family and I want to make sure that my family was took care of. It's something you can just send down to generation to generation. … I got children. My uncles has got sons that's coming up. That way we can just pass it down." Emma intends to keep the business going long enough for the next generation to step in and continue the family legacy.

Others are less sure whether and when they will pass down the family traditions. Jina explains that one day she will pass on the traditional recipes that are not written down, such as how to make kimchi, to her daughter, but not for a while: "When she gets older and when she gets married, then I will teach her." Jina sees marriage as an important marker for passing on traditional recipes. Yeon, another kimchi maker in Houston, explains why marriage is such an important marker for learning to make kimchi: "All Koreans pretty much naturally know how to make it. If you are a Korean housewife, then you learn how to make it." Yeon learned how to make kimchi from her mother "after I got married, at 26 years old. That's when I started." She explains her hesitation to pass on the tradition:

> Making kimchi looks simple, but it's very complex, so I don't really want to teach the younger ones. These days people just buy it for convenience. I'm willing to teach those of the younger generation who want to learn ... but I don't want to force on the tradition to those who don't want to learn.

The decision to pass down traditional recipes depends not only on gendered expectations of women's roles that do not commence until marriage, but also on the younger generation's ability to push back against those cultural expectations even if it means losing traditional foodways.

Place-based foodways

The coastal communities of Virginia and North Carolina offer a specific case of the interwoven foodways that have played out as ethnic groups moved into the region and came into contact with Indigenous people and African-descended groups that have been in the region for hundreds of years. While ethnic foods have a long history in the US, other dishes represent the unique conditions of the South that placed ethnic groups into close contact over extended periods of time. Two examples of this blending are collard green sandwiches and yock, which are both dishes found along the Virginia and North Carolina coasts (Edge, 2017).

While the history of the Lumbee makes them distinct from Southern whites or blacks, their foodways closely parallel popular Southern dishes including regionally specific variations of barbecue. Eric describes the response he gets at his family's barbecue restaurant from customers who are not familiar with eastern North Carolina foodways: "They're looking for—especially travelers—barbecue covered with the thick sauce and stuff, and that's not us. ... I try to explain to them we don't do it like that. We like the flavor of the meat." Instead, his restaurant uses his father's recipe for a vinegar-based sauce common to the eastern portion of the state. He describes the joy he sees in customers when they try his food:

> We don't use canned stuff. It's all frozen stuff or fresh stuff. ... I love to see people like that, 'cause you can just see the reaction on their face when they go to tasting it, they hadn't never tasted Southern country cooking like that 'cause we still cook like my grandma and them cooked. I reckon that's the reason it's still tasting like you're at home, especially in this area. That's the way I was raised up, the way we cook now.

Eric remembers growing up on his family's 100-year-old farm, when trips to the store were reserved for sugar and flour. Today, he tries to bring that sense of home and the original farm-to-table cooking to his customers. Although many of these dishes are common across the South, they are also traditional Lumbee dishes.

The collard green sandwich is another popular Lumbee dish that can be found in Lumbee homes as well as at some festivals. Glenn describes when he and his wife started selling the sandwiches at festivals:

> We cut up a bunch of collards and went down there one year at the Powwow—not the Homecoming but the Powwow—and sold a lot of collards. We had about 75, 80 gallons. ... We didn't have no idea it was going to enlarge like it is, but God just blessed us through all that.

He explains that even though the collards are increasingly popular, not everyone knows what a collard is: "They thought it was spinach. They hadn't never—they know nothing about a collard. So, you have a lot of folks that don't know nothing about collards. When you come [here] though, ask any neighbor or anybody, they can tell you about collards." A collard sandwich for Eric's family is collard greens placed between two thin pieces of cornbread with a piece of fatback. While some people do not know what a collard green is, Eric notes that others recognize the fundamental link between collards and the region: "People love collards in this area. ... And 'cause when we have like Homecoming, Fourth of July, Pembroke at the parade, there's some booths and they sell a lot of collard sandwiches. People love collard sandwiches, but I was raised up on collard sandwiches." The prevalence of collard greens in the region can be linked to the importance of farming and having a garden that often includes collards. Glenn explains the importance of farming traditions in the local community:

> We basically do our own stuff. That's the way we live around here. And you have to do that to survive. A lot of people don't know that, they throwed their heritage away. ... But we know this stuff. We're left with all this knowledge from our ancestors. We're trying to give it to these kids, but they don't want to know nothing about it now. My granddaughter there, she's catching on pretty good if I can just get that computer out of her hand.

The agricultural traditions in the area are still a major part of life. Although the sandwich began as a money-making endeavor born of frugality and industrialization as the Lumbee began selling sandwiches to workers at the local textile factory, today the sandwich is a mainstay on the menu during celebrations (Edge, 2017).

The local waterways, similar to the local agriculture, also shape the region's foodways. Emma describes the most popular fish she sells at her fish market: "[Spots], a well-known fish around here. That people's favorite fish is a croaker or a spot, but particularly people love spots. ... [Fried with Old Bay]'s pretty much an Indian style. That's the way they would normally do it." Although she buys fish from a seafood purveyor or sources it from the water off the Virginia and North Carolina coasts, she also cleans the fish that locals catch and continues to practice the traditional Lumbee way of cooking fish.

Yock has a complex history in Virginia. Chinese restaurants were often located in African American neighborhoods and were frequented by members of the community, largely because they were among the few public spaces where blacks were welcomed during the Jim Crow era. By the first half of the 1900s, blacks comprised a majority of the clientele in Chinese restaurants (Chen, 2014). Over time in the Tidewater region of Virginia, the lines between Chinese yock and the African American community blurred. Jenny explains how she understands the history of yock in Virginia:

> Yock became popular in the African American neighborhoods because that is where many of the Chinese immigrants opened their restaurants. Pizza in Italy is very different than the pizza in the US, but everyone know that pizza originated in Italy. Yock is originally a Chinese dish but it has been given a new identity by the African American community.

Jenny's father owned one of the first noodle companies that made yock-a-mein, the noodle traditionally used in yock. Today, yock is popular in the African American community and has become a staple dish in many area restaurants. Patsy explains why her restaurant started serving yock in the 1960s:

> The yock and the sausage, we've been selling that since 1965. In the beginning the restaurant was mostly more of American sandwiches like fish sandwiches, hotdogs, and hamburgers. After that, when the fast food restaurants came around, we served more of the yock, fried rice, egg foo-yang, lo-mein, those. And this restaurant is more like an old-fashioned basic Chinese. ... People were going for more authentic or simple, that why they come to us.

The ability to claim authentic Chinese traditions through their simplicity and opposition to mainstream American fast food options has made Patsy's restaurant successful.

Bernice reminisces about her time working at the Horseshoe, a local Suffolk, Virginia restaurant, known for yock, that was opened by a Japanese immigrant in the late 1930s, then sold to a black woman in 1945: "When I started working there it was African American. ... We had Southern fried chicken, fish, pork chops, liver and onions, chitlins, all of the good stuff, and the yock." The restaurant was popular among the factory workers, as she explains: "We had the white folks but not Chinese. We had a lot of white customers." Her friend, Mary, elaborates: "The white customer mainly came from the department stores downtown and the courthouses." Although yock is a Chinese dish, members of the African American community have put their own spin on the dish, and most people including Mary and Bernice do not recall seeing any Chinese communities in the area until the

1970s. Today, Mary and Bernice make yock for church and community fundraisers, and the media attention they have garnered, first from local newspapers, then larger regional papers, has brought a wide variety of customers from around the region:

> When she wrote the article up the next month, we had so many Caucasians coming to purchase and calling. Now when we have it, we put it in the paper and we got a standing number of Caucasian that we have to call them and they come they get five, ten [boxes] at a time.

Although the Horseshoe was owned by an African American couple, their son, John, describes his parents' notable stance on integration in the 1940s, when theirs was one of the only restaurants where African Americans could go for a sit-down meal:

> My parents didn't look at that. The chief of police would bring his family there and some Caucasian ministers would bring their family and some people did complain and said, "Look, we can't go to their restaurant and eat, why do you let them?" My parents said, "Look, this is a business. You know integration is coming. Whenever it comes, you know it's going to come. So, we don't stop people from eating because of that." And they respected that.

The history of yock presents a unique case of a Chinese dish that became a staple in African American restaurants and served a diverse customer base in the Jim Crow South. As John T. Edge (2017) argues, the blended South is the modern South, and it extends far beyond the stereotypical black and white foodways of the pre-Civil War era to a more racially diverse food history that includes Mexican, Chinese, and Arabic immigrants as well as Indigenous groups whose foodways pre-date the arrival of European colonists. Although numerous groups call the South home, tensions still arise around claims of what counts as authentic Southern food, detracting from the reality of Southern foodways as a diverse set of regional foodways that are constantly evolving to reflect the many changes among the region's communities.

Conclusion

Across the South, ethnic and regional foodways offer an alternative to the traditional, and often stereotypical, understandings of Southern food. Whether tamales in Mississippi, collard green sandwiches in Lumberton, North Carolina, or yock in the Tidewater region of Virginia, there is a complex interplay between racial and ethnic groups around foodways that represent alternatives to what is seen as Southern food, or the Americanized versions of ethnic foodways that erase the complexities of place-based foodways for immigrants as well as those who have been in the same place for generations. The complexity embedded in Southern foodways offers insight into the racial experiences in the South. Although they do experience discrimination, these family-owned restaurants and grocers appeal to a diverse clientele willing and often eager to seek out authentic food experiences beyond Americanized and white-washed dishes. These establishments offer important opportunities throughout the South as well, including the opportunity for the next generation to receive a college education, start a business of their own, or possibly continue the family legacy through the restaurant or grocery store. They also provide the opportunity to bring diverse, segregated communities together by highlighting a unique, blended variation of ethnic and Southern foodways. Considered together, these families and their establishments showcase the importance of food in everyday life that eschews stereotypes and exists as an art form of sustenance, a long legacy of crafting meals from multiple heritages that provide a lens into the complex cultural contours of the South that families must navigate each day.

Conclusion: The Future of Southern Food

The food on our plates is not disconnected from the mechanisms of social stratification and inequality. Who picks the food, cooks the food, eats the food, and pays for the food are all part of this intertwined, unequal system. This concluding chapter places Southern foodways and the inequality embedded in traditional representations of it into conversation regarding the increasing media and tourist attention garnered by popular Southern foods. While advantageous to some producers, these trends reinforce the financial hardships along with the many racial, ethnic, and gendered stereotypes faced by others who are integral to these foodways and traditions. This final chapter explores the diversity embedded in Southern foodways if we choose to look beyond the popular stereotypes, while also considering some of the larger societal changes in the restaurant industry sparked by the coronavirus pandemic.

Across each chapter the producers of craft food and beverages in the South have been shown to be grounded in the history of their industry and in place itself. History is important, whether it is geographical as in the case of Virginia and North Carolina winemakers recalling Thomas Jefferson's goal to make wine on par with those being produced in France at the time and Sir Walter Raleigh's planting of muscadine grapes, or family history as in the case of farmers and shrimpers who are the current generation in a long line of family members to make their lives on the land or water. In both cases, the importance of place, or terroir, permeates the decision-making process surrounding what products to grow that will thrive in the South.

It is this grounding in place and possibilities for the future, coupled with the South's new image as a cosmopolitan destination, that is drawing people from across the country to call the South home or to visit the region. These consumers may bring with them their own preconceived notions of the South, often reflecting narrow historical and literal black and white racial divisions, or they may come to the region viewing it as a commercialized tourist destination that takes the racial and class history of the South and makes it palatable to outsiders by offering that history for sale in quaint shops across the Southern states, selling symbols of an exotic or tranquil past for a small price (Cox, 2008). This is achieved by instilling a false collective memory that shapes the identity of the South through both the erasure and the reclamation of selective parts of the past (Huber, 2008).

Yet the South tourists see is no longer black and white, if indeed it ever was. Today, the South is home to a diverse group of people from around the world, and each group has brought along their own traditions and foodways (Jones, 2019). These traditions appear throughout the region, from Mexican restaurants in Kentucky to Indian restaurants in Arkansas and Chinese restaurants in Texas. These restaurants all move beyond classical understandings of Southern food to offer consumers a variety of ethnic cuisines grounded in the chefs' taste memories of their country of origin but with the inclusion of local products, such as Kentucky-grown and milled corn in the fresh tortillas served daily at one of the Mexican restaurants, where the chef prides herself on replicating the tastes from her grandmother's kitchen.

Southern food has never been static. From the earliest days of Southern history, colonists learned how to maintain the taste memories they had brought with them from England with the products that were available in the New World. Years later, slaves integrated African foodways through ingredients and cooking techniques, such as the use of okra as a thickening agent in gumbo, into now iconic Southern dishes. Today, immigrants continue to bring their foodways into the region and further alter the meaning of Southern food to include dishes such as tamales, popular in Mississippi, but not the same as the tamales that are found in Mexico. Instead, the tamales found across Mississippi are smaller and made from corn meal, not corn flour, and they are simmered then served with their cooking liquid. Southern food will continue to change to reflect the people who call the region home. Although Southern food has received increasing national recognition, largely focused on the award-winning, often male, chefs of Charleston, New Orleans, and Atlanta, it would be inaccurate to assume authentic Southern food is only found in those locations. Although these chefs and cities have dominated Southern food for most of recent memory, a subtle change is coming to Southern food, and its makers are women and men of color from the South and around the world who are increasingly being recognized on the national stage for their contributions to modern Southern food.

In 2018, the James Beard Award for Best Chef Southeast, one of the highest awards in the US food industry, went to Rodney Scott. His recognition with the prestigious award was monumental for two reasons. First, he is a black pitmaster who was recognized by an elite restaurant industry that is still overwhelmingly white. It should also be noted that in the same year, chef Michael Twitty's (2017) *The Cooking Gene*, which explores the history of African diasporic foodways in the historical South, won the James Beard Award for Book of the Year, and Nina Compton, a Saint Lucian chef in New Orleans won the award for Best Chef South. Second, Rodney Scott won the Best Chef Southeast award by cooking traditional barbecue, setting him far apart from the five other fine dining restaurants that were nominated alongside him, including the tastemaker restaurant at Blackberry Farms, which has received countless recognitions. The 2018 James Beard Awards marked a shift in culinary prestige, as several women and people of color took home awards that historically have gone to white men cooking in fine dining restaurants. The 2018 awards went to chefs who were cooking great food: barbecue, classic Southern pastries including peach cobbler, Asian egg tarts, and Caribbean food (Purvis, 2018). Although not all these chefs are located in the South, the move toward more culinary acceptance and diversity at the prestigious James Beard Awards suggests the culinary industry as a whole may be moving toward inclusivity for both cuisines and the people who prepare them.

The success of the restaurateurs who won prizes at the 2018 James Beard Awards, and of the craft food producers discussed throughout this book, lies at the intersection of two main concepts. First, in their dedication to their craft, these producers, whether the early Virginia winemakers pursuing their goal of producing great wines from Virginia soil in the 1970s despite pushback from the local universities and extension agents or the pig farmers who provide Rodney Scott with the pork he uses at his barbecue restaurant, are all carrying on Southern food traditions and are motivated by far more than the desire to seek out an alternative to a white-collar desk job, as commonly mentioned by craft producers in New York City (Ocejo, 2017). While the success of these craft producers is largely dependent on a consumer base that is willing to pay more for craft products, whether because they think they taste better, as in the case of heirloom vegetables (Jordan, 2015), or because of the social status conveyed by consuming them among groups such as "foodies" (Johnston and Baumann, 2010), few of these producers have received financial profits that would justify the hard work involved. Frequently the hard work was cited as a deterrent for the next generation entering into the business because profit could not be the main motivating factor—it had to be a passion for the work itself.

Second, as Michael Borer (2019) found with craft brewers in Las Vegas, the production of craft products is a combination of science and art aimed at achieving an authentic product. As previously discussed, authenticity is the process of careful impression management on the part of the producers to ensure consumers believe they are consuming a "true" product that is grounded in a sincere and original representation. They are seeking to eat the "real thing." The science and art involved in safely canning vegetables or curing country ham should not be ignored in favor of discussions of how one product is more or less authentic than a competitor's product, for example. All these producers share knowledge and skills required for their craft that should be valued as art, not only as food (Fantasia, 2010), and looking at those similarities offers insights into the meanings embedded in Southern food and reveals the divergences between industries.

Shared craft

Although this book spans five different Southern food industries (winemaking, fishing, farming, curing, and restaurants and grocers), there are a few recurring themes that weave these groups of producers and purveyors together. The first theme relates to the producers' roles as small craft industries, and subsequently their vulnerability to the whims of consumers and nature. The second relates to the producers' literal grounding in a specific place and the taste memories associated with that place. Finally, each producer engages with some form of invisibility or marginality on the part of either themselves or others in their industry.

The dichotomy between heritage and modern identity and production methods occurs across all five industries. All the business owners discussed in this book represent small, often family-owned endeavors, existing by definition in opposition to their large industrial counterparts. Some of the owners represent large businesses in their region or specific industry; for example, Barboursville Vineyard is one of the largest wineries in Virginia and the largest in the Monticello AVA, but it is still owned by the original family, unlike many of its California counterparts that have been sold to large conglomerates (Conaway, 2018). These businesses, some a few years old and others going back to the early 1900s, all represent small business models whose success is dependent on their identity as craft and local businesses and their ability to maintain a balance between traditional techniques and modern technologies.

In every case, the techniques involved in these industries are not new, although technological advances have made possible new methods such as grafting grape vines and creating temperature-controlled rooms for curing country ham. The processes of shrimping, farming, and curing are all old traditions, but over time and as industrial agriculture became dominant, many of these practices became less common on the small business scale. For example, instead of canning jellies and pickles at home, most people buy them from the grocery store or a local farmers' market where they are sold as artisanal jellies. Yet the knowledge and art involved in canning fruits or baking from scratch can easily be lost, and it could be argued that they were lost for several generations who relied on the ease of commercially available foods to reduce the amount of time spent in the kitchen. This technology was critical for women entering the workforce and young adults delaying marriage, because they did not need to devote as much time to cooking or need someone to prepare their food when a microwave and a can could serve the same purpose (Coontz, 2006). However, as voiced throughout these oral histories, the processes embedded in the production of heritage foods are being maintained by a new generation interested in craft products and other nonindustrial food alternatives.

The second theme tying these industries together is the place-specific tastes that attract consumers seeking out authentic culinary experiences. Across all these industries, the producers are tapping into the edible or taste memory of a specific place. This appears in two key forms throughout the South. The first is the terroir, or the ability to taste a specific place in a finished product, such as pigs fed on acorns in the Appalachian Mountains or the area in which a wine is produced. The second is a specific taste memory connecting a person to a time in the past, such as the food from one's country of origin or a grandmother's table. These food memories can be heirloom ingredients, including freshly made tortillas, or processed foods, such as soy sauce made in Hong Kong that is unavailable in US markets. Both serve to connect the consumer to a specific taste memory, either one they have personally or one they wish to experience that belongs to the chef's personal history.

Taste, or edible, memories draw on the ability to use food as a vehicle to access the past. Unlike other cultural products, such as sculptures, that can exist in their unaltered form for centuries, food only lasts until it is consumed or begins to decompose. As sociologist Jennifer Jordan (2015) explains in her work on heirloom fruits and vegetables, edible memory is not isolated to an individual but guides people's actions to plant gardens, save seeds, and cook meals, as well as to tell stories about the food and the past. As evidenced in the experience of immigrants who had trouble finding specific vegetables or spices that were common in their country of origin, the ability to recreate a taste of place became increasingly valuable, especially in their restaurants. While many recalled being forced to adapt their cuisine, whether because of fishing laws that limit the number of shad caught off North Carolina waters or the unavailability of bok choy or epazote in US grocery stores, the determination of chefs and producers to maintain their culinary memories while adapting to what is available is a recurring success story of how marginalized cultures adapt to life in the US until the market catches up with consumer demand, as in the case of dried chiles that were once uncommon except in Mexico and along the US Southwestern border (Pilcher, 2012).

The unavailability of certain ingredients, and the subsequent negotiation on the part of the cook to produce a familiar dish without the familiar ingredients, reflects the third theme running throughout these oral histories: the dual invisibility of the people. At various points in time, all the producers have coped with the invisibility of their position, from the early Virginia winemakers who were discouraged by state agricultural leaders to the Gulf Coast shrimpers who are still coping with the devastation caused by poor corporate decision-making, resulting in the BP oil spill and subsequent government decision to flush fresh water into the marsh system and to use a chemical dispersant. These groups, as with the restaurant industry in general, often represent members of the lower class whose occupations are vulnerable to changes in government regulation or broader market fluctuations. For example, these challenges include the use of turtle excluders that can allow valuable shrimp to escape fishermen's nets, or farmers, who already have slim profit margins, facing a late frost that causes the loss of an entire season's worth of a crop, such as when a polar vortex caused grape buds across the Midwest and South to freeze on the night of May 8, 2020, causing a substantial drop in wine production for the year (McKee, 2020).

Although the industries as a whole endure structural disadvantages brought on by both natural events and human decisions, participants in the industries are often unaware of the social inequalities within their industries. Across all the industries race, class, and gender only occasionally entered conversations, and in many cases it was almost as a side note. Jobs in these industries, as in the restaurant industry itself, are often low paid with minimal benefits, and many women and people of color experience discrimination in the professional kitchen, typically a white male-dominated space (Harris and Giuffre, 2015; Lippert, Rosing, and Tendick-Matesanz, 2020). One notable exception is evident in the Mississippi shrimpers' comments regarding the arrival of Vietnamese refugees who entered the fishing industry, which was often discussed as a historical example of experiences with the changing demographics of a specific place and industry. The difficulties of their shared profession meant the shrimpers were accepted, while the government policies that were seen as favoring the Vietnamese shrimpers over white shrimpers remained a point of contention (Omi and Winant, 2015; Bonilla-Silva, 2017). Meanwhile, many of the ethnic restaurant owners recounted experiences with discrimination but framed them as isolated experiences rather than systemic problems.

While race was minimally discussed, the role of gender across the industries was talked about more openly among the oral history participants. In the case of each industry, at least a portion of time was spent acknowledging the role of women within these traditionally male-dominated occupations. In many cases women operated alongside their husbands in the family-owned business, but some women, including Felicia of Oakencroft Winery and Nancy from Colonel Newsom's country ham business, not only ran their businesses without male partners but were leaders in their industries. The role of gender in the food industry has long been a point of contention, with women being held responsible for domestic food production as part of their unpaid household labor while men are visible in the public sphere of professional kitchens and other food production industries (Harris and Giuffre, 2015). While race and gender were discussed only sparingly, class was a recurring issue across places and occupations, as many families turned to food production for the additional income or invested heavily in the necessary equipment, such as a shrimp boat, to perform their tasks. All these industries are vulnerable to natural and human-made disasters that can cause financial devastation, for example through the loss of a boat because of a hurricane's violent winds or heavy rains that wash away newly planted crops. Many of these business owners are operating with slim profit margins, and the threat of going out of business after a bad season is a common source of anxiety. This anxiety is also a driving factor among parents to encourage their children to pursue other, seemingly more stable occupations, or at least to obtain a college degree before entering the industry.

The impression of craft

Across all three of these themes underlies the theoretical framing that guides this book and makes it possible to look at craft consumption with a critical lens. The success of craft food depends on the separation of the front and backstage of life, with consumers occupying the often elegant or relaxed front stage of farmers' markets, local meat markets, and winery tasting rooms, and producers present backstage on the farms, vineyards, and fishing boats, catching or growing the products that are served on the front stage. As many of the shrimpers mentioned, fishing is inherently dangerous, and many have seen the horror of what happens when something goes wrong at sea. However, few consumers think about the risks involved in fishing when they are consuming fresh seafood.

As sociologist Richard Peterson (1997) found in his in-depth study of country music, the appearance of a cultural product as authentic is largely dependent on the producer or singer being seen as a real or legitimate representation of what consumers believe a country music singer should look, talk, and act like, in addition to the songs being original to the singer and not reproductions of existing songs, but still grounded in accepted country music themes and sounds. This is the work of a team of producers, stylists, and marketing agencies who create an image of the singer; even if that image is fabricated, so it can be read by the consumer as authentic. While these constraints reflect the distinctions between the front and backstage in which the producer engages in impression management to ensure the consumer is unaware of the production realities (Hughes, 2000), claims of authenticity are not without their own politics, because claiming authenticity inherently means claiming value and creating distinctions of inequality, where one product may be branded as inferior to another and thus lose value. In the case of craft foods, their authenticity is embedded in claims that they are sincere and original dishes or ingredients that exist in opposition to their industrially produced, or in the case of craft beer conglomerate-owned, counterparts (Peterson, 1997; Borer, 2019).

Similar to country music, the maintenance of authenticity requires constant attention beyond the interpersonal level outlined by Goffman (1959), and instead occupies the structural level where the entire field of producers work together to create a final product that consumers believe is original and sincere (Peterson, 1997). As sociologist Michael Hughes (2000) argues, the fabrication of authenticity at the organizational level reflects the same process of impression management that occupies the interpersonal level. By analyzing the organizational level of culture, we can move toward overcoming the shortcomings of the production of culture approach in accounting for determining cultural meanings (Griswold, 1987; Hughes, 2000). The emphasis on the production of cultural products—country music in Richard Peterson's case, and Southern food culture in this book—shifts the focus of cultural meanings to how producers of cultural products determine their subsequent meaning. It is in this context of Goffman's impression management that the balance between the front and backstage becomes appropriate to understand how producers actively manage the meanings of the cultural products they produce, because authenticity is socially constructed, and its importance comes into play when authenticity is in doubt (Beverland, 2005; Peterson, 2005). The tensions are where authenticity exists, and the rapidly changing food scene keeps producers in constant tension with themselves, each other, consumers, and the media industry that sells narrow views of the products and processes that are seen as being the most authentic.

Imagine, briefly, waking up on a Saturday morning and grabbing a latte from the local coffee shop before walking a couple blocks to the neighborhood farmers' market, where you engage with local farmers and fill your reusable canvas bag with fresh heirloom tomatoes, brightly colored peppers, and juicy peaches before walking back to your home. Now, imagine having to pull weeds, till the dirt, and carefully watch for bugs or mold on your tomato plants all week, then waking up in the early hours of the morning the day before heading to the market because a thunderstorm is rolling in. Picking every ripe tomato is a necessity to avoid the financial loss that will be incurred if the rain from the storm causes the thin skin of those tomatoes to rupture or the wind knocks them off their vines. Once most of the tomatoes are saved, and you have put in another long day of work, you head to bed for a few hours before rising early once again to load your vehicle, drive to the market, and run your stand for the next six hours and talk with consumers as they buy the tomatoes you so carefully harvested the day before. This market represents the front stage, with a leisurely Saturday morning trip to the market and light conversation with farmers, while the backstage is represented by the farmer coping with the weather to make a profit on the tomatoes and telling the story of how the tomatoes made it to the customers' bags.

The farmers at the market work together to create the cultural meanings surrounding the heirloom fruits and vegetables that consumers enjoy. As with country music, the producers are not acting in isolation. Instead, as Goffman explains, interpersonal interactions that rely on the producer adjusting to consumers' reactions is central to creating these meanings around craft foods. Successful impression management allows the actors, or farmers, chefs, and purveyors in this case, to create a shared understanding or meaning of the situation (Hughes, 2000). Throughout this book, Southern food producers have been shown to work together, whether on the same dock, at the same farmers' market, or within a shared AVA, to give meaning to Southern food whose origins date back generations. However, like music, Southern food continues to evolve with each subsequent generation and changes in relation to six facets of cultural production: technology, regulations, industry and organizational structures, occupational careers, and market conditions (Peterson and Anand, 2004). Each of these facets were present in the oral histories discussed in the preceding chapters, and each can make or break family farms and businesses.

The future of Southern food in a post-pandemic society

"As bad as Katrina was, you knew that one day it would just be over. We'll clean up, we'll rebuild and get back to it. You know, this is a lot more unknown," Donald Link, a New Orleans restaurateur, explains in response to the pandemic's impact on the industry (Elliott, 2020). In March 2020, the coronavirus pandemic spread rapidly throughout the United States and the world. Restaurants across the US closed their doors and laid off hundreds of thousands of employees. Some of these restaurants noted that they were closing permanently, while others hoped to weather the storm and reopen at some point in the future. Farmers' markets were not able to open for spring sales because the design of the markets did not allow for physical distancing or "social distancing," a word that quickly entered the common vernacular that spring. Even grocery stores put in rationing policies, not seen in the US since the days of World War II, and commercials for "victory gardens" started appearing on television.

"Regardless of how trivial brewing a beer might be when compared to the grueling work of first responders and hospital workers, it still shows a way that people relate to the world with and through other people and cultural objects alike" (Borer, 2019, p 244). Although Borer is referring to the 2017 Las Vegas shooting that took the lives of 60 people, the statement continues to resonate in the midst of the pandemic. Food may be trivial as long as there is enough to eat, but the desire to reopen restaurants and spend time with friends and family around a table or grill is a popular refrain now that stay-at-home orders and social distancing put in place to limit the virus's spread have led to the closure of restaurants and the separation of friends and families. Food is embedded with meaning by both consumers and producers: whether these meanings are carefully managed impressions of authenticity and heirloom status or reminders of time spent with loved ones, the importance of food and the meanings behind it has been a recurring theme throughout the pandemic. The reopening of restaurants is frequently mentioned as one of the most important aspects of social life for which people are yearning.

As leading Southern food writer John T. Edge (2020) explains in an article published shortly after the virus shut down restaurants across the South, it is too soon to know what the future of the restaurant industry or the thousands of small businesses and producers that support it will look like in the coming months or years. Yet leading chefs in the restaurant industry, including Edward Lee and John Currence, are coming together to support their employees and working within their cities and states to ensure those in the industry who are out of work or quarantined with the virus have food and relative stability in these uncertain days. And leading Washington, DC, chef Jose Andres, who has been at the forefront of numerous disasters in recent years, providing food to people in hurricane-ravaged communities, turned his Michelin star restaurant into a soup kitchen, as well as converting the Nationals' baseball stadium into a field kitchen to distribute food (Kavilanz, 2020). Despite these efforts to feed those who are hungry and out of work, the restaurant industry, from the smallest roadside stand to the fine dining restaurants of Charleston, is being severely impacted by the pandemic. Edge (2020) notes: "Change is happening so fast. And, as we watch counts spike across the South, change is happening so slow. ... In previous times of crisis, Southerners gathered in restaurants to hatch recoveries or mourn losses. This crisis is different." At the time of writing, we do not know what the future will look like for the restaurant industry, with ongoing stay-at-home orders, social distancing, the threat of a second wave still in place, and everyone waiting for a reliable vaccine to calm the stormy waters of society. It's likely that some of the restaurateurs and producers discussed in this book will close their businesses permanently, but all hope is not lost, as many others weathered the Great Depression and several global recessions and will continue to fight for their existence for generations to come.

It is possible that, as Michael Borer (2019) discusses in his explanation of the success of the craft brewing industry in Las Vegas in the wake of the Great Recession, the coronavirus pandemic will lead many consumers to consider their local products and cultural scene as a viable investment. As states begin to reopen businesses and fear of a second wave of the virus cancels future travel plans, it is possible that as people lack the money or confidence to travel long distances, local areas will be given more attention, leading to a new local food movement. Another consequence of the pandemic is that discrimination against and hate crimes toward Asians and Asian Americans have increased, given that the virus is seen as originating from China and is derogatorily labeled as such by the media and leading politicians (Loffman, 2020). Although the focus is currently on the wrongful discrimination and hate crimes experienced by those who appear to look Asian, many Chinese restaurants have completely ceased operations as a result of the pandemic because their small operating margins have left them vulnerable, and a large portion of them will never reopen (Alcorn, 2020). This reality also means that the future of many of the businesses discussed throughout this book, whether the Vietnamese shrimpers along the Gulf Coast, the Asian restaurant owners in Texas, or the Chinese grocers across the South, is uncertain.

At this point, early predictions are that a quarter of the restaurants that closed because of COVID-19 will not be reopening their doors. The future remains uncertain as unemployment rates have skyrocketed and the US economy is headed toward a third recession in less than 20 years. The restaurant industry was already home to many low-income workers, who have now lost their jobs and are unlikely to find work again until the industry begins to recover, exposing existing gaps in society and increasing the level of inequality (Edge, 2020). The lasting effects of the pandemic are unknown, but the restaurant industry and the world will look different after the pandemic. However, there is still hope. Food rationing, skyrocketing unemployment rates, and economic contraction have all occurred before. People survived the Great Depression and emerged with a new understanding of the world and new social safety nets in place (Ziegelman and Coe, 2016). Although our world, and daily life in particular, will look different when the pandemic ends, food and the cultural meanings of it embedded in people's lives will not go away, even though those meanings may change.

Hope always provides solace and encouragement, even in the darkest of days. People can find hope through food and the fond memories and meanings they attach to it. Hoping for the perfect biscuit to start the day. Hoping for a meal among friends that lasts long into the night. Hoping for a glass of wine that reminds you of summer rainstorms cutting across humid hillsides. For now, I hope this time next year I will be able to make my way through downtown to a small, quirky neighborhood called Kerrytown to visit the farmers' market. Then, I'll walk across the street to Zingerman's Delicatessen and pick up some of Colonel Newsom's country ham that Nancy made deep in the hills of Kentucky to continue supporting the farmers and purveyors of these centuries-old Southern foodways. My hope is that many of these important communities, though often invisible and marginalized to many across the US, will survive and continue the heritage craft legacies that can be part of our lives for generations to come.

APPENDIX

Oral History Participants

Chapter 1: Winemakers, 18 Oral History Participants

Name	State	Age	Gender	Race/Ethnicity	Occupation	Generation
Dennis H.[1]	VA	63	M	White	Winery Owner	1st
Gabriele R.[1]	VA	–	F	Italian	Gardener/Vineyard	–
Felicia R.[1]	VA	–	F	White	Winery Owner	1st
Chris P.[1]	VA	47	M	English	Winery Owner	1st
Melissa C.[1]	VA	38	F	White	Winery Restaurant Chef	–
Robert T.[2]	GA	56	M	White	Winery Owner	
Charlie C.[2]	GA	–	M	White	Winery Owner	2nd
Charles C.[2]	GA	56	M	White	Winery Owner	1st
Mary Ann H.[2]	GA	40	F	White	Winery Owner	1st
Willard H.[1]	NC	–	M	White	Winery Owner/Dentist (R)	1st
Bob H.[1]	NC	–	M	White	Winery Owner	2nd
Bo W.[1]	NC	59	M	White	Winery Owner/Power Company (R)	1st
Sonya W.[1]	NC	–	F	White	Winery Owner	1st
Dave F.[1]	NC	40	M	White	Winery Owner	2nd
Jerry D.[2]	NC	57	M	White	Winery Manager	–
Lenna H.[1]	NC	64	F	White	Winery Owner	1st
Frank H.[1]	NC	65	M	White	Winery Owner	1st
Lillian[1]	NC	–	F	White	Winery Owner	–

R: Retired, [1] Interview by Amy C. Evans, [2] Interview by John T. Edge

Chapter 2: Saltwater, 56 Oral History Participants

Name	State	Age	Gender	Race/Ethnicity	Occupation	Generation
Leroy D.[1]	MS	64	M	White	Shrimper (R)	1st
Frank P.[1]	MS	35	M	White	Shrimper (R)	7th
Corky H.[1]	MS	86	M	Croatian	Shrimper (R)	2nd
Georgio T.[1]	MS	52	M	Croatian	Chef	–
Todd R.[1]	MS	37	M	Croatian	Processing/Sales	3rd
Peter N.[1]	MS	40	M	Vietnamese	Researcher	–
Richard G.[1]	MS	64	M	White	Processing/Sales	3rd
Sammy M.[1]	MS	53	M	Croatian	Shrimper/Boat Builder	3rd
George T.[2]	LA	64	M	White	Shrimper (R)/ Processing/Sales	1st
Carol T.[2]	LA	61	F	White	Shrimper (R)/ Processing/Sales	1st
Donald P.[2]	LA	–	M	White	Shrimper (R)/ Processing/Sales	1st
Melinda P.[2]	LA	54	F	White	Sales	1st
Pierre A.[2]	LA	40	M	White	Shrimper/Trapper	2nd
Wayne E.[2]	LA	62	M	White	Dock Owner (R)	2nd
Donna E.[2]	LA	60	F	White	Dock Owner (R)	2nd
Alphonnse C.[2]	LA	52	M	White	Fisherman/Bait Shop Owner	2nd
Marvin A.[2]	LA	50	M	White	Push Pole Maker/ Net Maker	3rd
Nick C.[2]	LA	41	M	White	Oysterman	4th
Mark C.[2]	LA	53	M	White	Offshore Supply Boat Worker/ Public Relations	–
Lawrence T.[2]	LA	71	M	White	Net Maker	1st
Robert C.[2]	LA	52	M	White	Processing/Sales	3rd
Raymond F.[2]	LA	60	M	White	Fisherman	–
Alzina T.[2]	LA	83	F	White	Chef	–
Donna C.[2]	LA	39	F	White	Chef/Restaurant Owner	–

(continued)

Name	State	Age	Gender	Race/Ethnicity	Occupation	Generation
Paul A.[3]	LA	–	M	White	Community Gardener	–
Pete G.[3]	LA	–	M	White	Fisherman/Sales	–
Clara G.[3]	LA	–	F	White	Fisherman/Sales	–
William B.[4]	VA	54	M	White	Chef/Restaurant Owner	–
Ashley S.[4]	VA	34	F	Pamunkey	Director, Pamunkey Museum and Cultural Center	–
Susan M.[4,5]	VA	70	F	White	Crabber (R)	–
Susan H.[5]	VA	68	F	White	Restaurant Owner	–
Charles W.[4]	VA	81	M	White	NASA (R)/ Volunteer Chef	–
Mary W.[4]	VA	82	F	White	NASA (R)/ Volunteer Chef	–
Kevin G.[4,5]	VA	46	M	White	Fisherman	2nd
Richard C.[4]	VA	61	M	White	Chef	–
William B.[6]	SC	70	M	White	Shrimper (R)	–
Kimberly C.[6]	SC	52	F	White	Crabber (R)/Sales	1st
Rocky M.[6]	SC	38	M	White	Shrimper	3rd
Andrew M.[6]	SC	76	M	White	Shrimper (R)	2nd
David T.[6]	SC	46	M	White	Fisherman	3rd
Anuruck S.[6]	SC	65	M	Thai	Fisherman	–
Nathaniel M.[6]	SC	74	M	Black	Crabber/Sales	1st
Fred D.[6]	SC	50	M	French	Fisherman	1st
Jamie W.[6]	SC	35	M	Black	Oysterman/ Crabber	2nd
Ellie B.[6]	SC	46	F	White	Processing/Sales	2nd
Joanie C.[6]	SC	46	F	White	Processing/Sales	2nd
Neal C.[6]	SC	53	M	White	Fisherman/Sales	2nd
Julie M.[6]	SC	50	F	White	Oyster Woman/ Clamming	2nd
Eddie W.[7,8]	NC	50	M	White	Fisherman	4th

(continued)

Name	State	Age	Gender	Race/Ethnicity	Occupation	Generation
Ira L.[7]	NC	98	M	White	Coast Guard (R)/ Charter Fishing Guide	–
Emma G.[7,8]	NC	83	F	White	Fisherman	2nd
Sarah G.[7,8]	NC	77	F	White	Cook/Cookbook Author	–
Mila G.[7,8]	NC	56	F	White	Restaurant Owner	1st
Makeley L.[7,8]	NC	91	M	White	Fisherman	2nd
Randy W.[7,8]	NC	41	M	White	Fisherman	3rd
Jan G.[7,8]	NC	77	F	White	Cookbook Contributor	–

[1] Interview by Francis Lam, [2] Interview by Sarah Roahen, [3] Interview by Laura Westbrook, [4] Interview by Jessica Taylor, [5] Interview by Patrick Daglaris, [6] Interview by Sara Wood, [7] Interview by Keia Mastrianni, [8] Interview by Mike Moore

Chapter 3: Farmers, 38 Oral History Participants

Name	State	Age	Gender	Race/Ethnicity	Occupation	Generation
Cecilia G.[1]	GA	40	F	Kenyan	Urban Farmer	3rd
Jamila N.[1]	GA	41	F	Jamaican/ Trinidadian	Urban Farmer	1st★
Susan P.[1]	GA	–	F	White	Refugee Farmer	1st
Celia B.[1]	GA	38	F	White	Organic Farmer	1st
Jenny J.[1]	GA	31	F	White	Farmer	2nd
Lauren C.[1]	GA	29	F	Filipino	Farmer	1st★
Jenni H.[1]	GA	26	F	White	Farmer	5th
Isia C.[2]	GA	36	F	White	Urban Farmer	1st
Charlotte S.[1]	GA	41	F	White	Farmer	1st
Erin C.[1]	GA	32	F	White	Urban Farmer	1st
Helen D.[1]	GA	77	F	Austrian	Organic Farmer	1st
Rebecca W.[1]	GA	30	F	White	Cheesemaker	1st
Ross W.[1]	GA	31	M	White	Farmer	1st
Judith W.[1]	GA	39	F	White	Farmer	3rd
Joe R.[1]	GA	35	M	White	Farmer	1st
Haylene G.[1]	GA	68	F	Jamaican	Urban Farmer	1st★
Leroy K.[3]	MS	–	M	Black	FM Participant	–

(continued)

Name	State	Age	Gender	Race/Ethnicity	Occupation	Generation
Elizabeth H.[4]	MS	40	F	White	Farmer/Chef	1st
John A.[3]	MS	59	M	White	Blueberry Farmer	–
Leann H.[3]	MS	56	F	White	Farmer	3rd
Donald B.[3]	MS	44	M	White	Baker (FM)	–
Alisa L.[3]	MS	55	F	White	Preserver (FM)	4th
Hal F.[3]	MS	58	M	White	Farmer	3rd
Hallie S.[3]	MS	65	F	Black	Farmer	3rd
Ben B.[5]	NC	58	M	White	Chef/ Restaurant Owner	–
Karen B.[5]	NC	54	F	White	Chef/ Restaurant Owner	–
April M.[5]	NC	34	F	White	Baker/ Preserver (FM)	–
Elise M.[5]	NC	36	F	White	Farmer	–
Wilma H.[5]	NC	–	F	White	Seed Saver (FM)	–
Marjorie O.[5]	NC	81	F	White	Farmer	2nd
Louise P.[6]	NC	–	F	Black	Baker (FM)	–
Michael B.[5]	NC	–	M	White	Farmer	3rd
Alex H.[5]	NC	55	M	White	Farmer	1st★
Betsy H.[5]	NC	55	F	White	Farmer	1st★
Sarah B.[6]	NC	28	F	White	FM Manager	–
Bill D.[6]	NC	66	M	White	Farmer	1st
Shelia N.[7]	NC	40	F	White	Chef/ Restaurant Owner	1st
Matt N.[7]	NC	40	M	White	Chef/ Restaurant Owner	1st

★ Although there may be farming traditions, they were not commercial
Urban means located within Atlanta City Limits
FM: farmers' market participant, not a farmer

[1] Interview by Sara Wood, [2] Interview by Jenna Mobley and Bang Tran, [3] Interview by Amy C. Evans, [4] Interview by Amy Evans Streeter, [5] Interview by Kate Medley, [6] Interview by Ashley Rose Young, [7] Interview by Sara Camp Arnold

Chapter 4: Curing, 19 Oral History Participants

Name	State	Age	Gender	Race	Occupation	Generation
Sydney M.[1]	VA	63	M	White	Restaurant Owner	3rd
Ron T.[1]	VA	51	M	White	Curemaster	2nd
Sam E. III[1]	VA	49	M	White	Curemaster	3rd
Allan B.[1]	TN	67	M	White	Curemaster	3rd
Rufus B[1]	NC	47	M	White	Plant Manager	2nd
Sally E.[1]	NC	62	F	White	Owner	2nd
Charles H.[1]	NC	44	M	White	Culinary Leader	–
Ronny D.[2]	KY	47	M	White	Curemaster	1st
Beth D.[2]	KY	46	F	White	Curemaster	1st
Rodman M.[2]	KY	52	M	White	Curemaster	2nd
William M.[2]	KY	92	M	White	Curemaster (R)	1st
Charles G. Jr[2]	KY	53	M	White	Curemaster	2nd
Lorene G.[2]	KY	85	F	White	Curemaster (R)	1st
Lewis S.[1]	KY	60	M	White	Curemaster	3rd
Jay D.[1]	KY	37	M	White	Curemaster	1st
Gregg R.[1]	KY	–	M	White	Professor	–
Nancy N.[2]	KY	50	F	White	Curemaster	3rd
Leslie S.[2]	KY	62	M	White	Farmer	3rd
June S.[2]	KY	–	F	White	Curemaster	3rd

[1] Interview by Sara Wood, [2] Interview by Amy C. Evans

Chapter 5: Restaurants, 48 Oral History Participants

Name	State	Age	Gender	Race/Ethnicity	Occupation	Generation
Dorsey H.[1]	NC	–	F	Lumbee	Ice Cream Maker	–
Glenn H.[1]	NC	61	M	Lumbee	Ice Cream Maker	–
Eric L.[1]	NC	47	M	Lumbee	BBQ Restaurant Owner	2nd
Emma L.[1]	NC	36	F	Lumbee	Fish Market Owner	2nd
Callie L.[1]	NC	72	F	Lumbee	General Store Owner	1st

(continued)

Name	State	Age	Gender	Race/Ethnicity	Occupation	Generation
Heaverd O.[1]	NC	76	M	Lumbee	Restaurant Owner	1st
Ajay P.[2]	TX	35	M	Indian	Restaurant Owner	1st
Yeon L.[2]	TX	71	F	Korean	Kimchi Maker	-
Jina K.[2]	TX	-	F	Korean	Restaurant Owner	1st
Jacklyn P.[2]	TX	35	F	Vietnamese	Restaurant Owner	2nd
Cori X.[2]	TX	29	M	Chinese	Restaurant Owner	1st
Heng C.[2]	TX	28	F	Chinese	Restaurant Owner	1st
Sue P.[2]	TX	56	F	Indian	Restaurant Owner	1st
Lawrence A.[2]	TX	54	M	White	Restaurant Owner	1st
Noi A.[2]	TX	41	F	Thai	Restaurant Owner	1st
Araceli C.[3]	KY	-	F	Mexican	Restaurant Owner	1st
Sandra M.[3]	KY	-	F	Romanian	Restaurant Worker	1st
Rosa S.[3]	KY	-	F	Mexican	Restaurant Owner	1st
Fabian L.[4]	KY	-	M	Mexican	Restaurant Owner	2nd
Laura R.[4]	KY	47	F	Mexican	Restaurant Owner	1st
Montzerat C.[3]	KY	26	F	Mexican	Restaurant Owner	1st
Luis M.[3]	KY	-	M	Mexican	Restaurant Owner	1st
Jesus M.[4]	KY	44	M	Mexican	Restaurant Owner	1st
Izmene P.[4]	KY	39	F	Mexican	Restaurant Owner	1st
Francisco B.[4]	KY	53	M	Mexican	Restaurant Manager	-

(continued)

Name	State	Age	Gender	Race/Ethnicity	Occupation	Generation
John D.[1]	VA	78	M	Black/Native American.	Restaurant Owner	2nd
Bernice C.[1]	VA	69	F	Black	Volunteer Chef	-
Mary W.[1]	VA	59	F	Black	Volunteer Chef	-
Jenny W.[1]	VA	63	F	Chinese	Noodle Company Owner	2nd
Patsy W.[1]	VA	62	F	Chinese	Restaurant Owner	2nd
Raymond W.[5]	MS	58	M	Chinese	Grocer	2nd
Tony L.[5]	MS	62	M	Chinese	Grocer	1st
Monica L.[5]	MS	54	F	Chinese	Grocer	1st
Luck W.[5]	MS	81	M	Chinese	Grocer	2nd
Frieda Q.[5]	MS	68	F	Chinese	Grocer	2nd
Sue N.[6]	MS	32	F	Vietnamese	Baker	1st
Joe Dan Y.[5]	AR	56	M	Chinese	Grocer	2nd
Arun S.[7]	AR	-	M	Indian	Restaurant Owner	1st
Satish S.[7]	AR	61	M	Indian	Restaurant Owner	1st
Ali M.[7]	AR	48	M	Jordanian	Restaurant Owner	1st
Sreepathy, H.[7]	AR	-	F	Indian	Restaurant Owner	1st
Ravi P.[7]	AR	26	M	Indian	Restaurant Manager	1st
Maya S.[7]	AR	-	F	Indian	Restaurant Owner	1st
Sayed A.[7]	AR	-	M	Indian	Restaurant Owner	1st
Naidu M.[7]	AR	-	M	Indian	Restaurant Owner	1st
Lisa P.[7]	AR	61	F	White	Restaurant Owner	1st
Abhijeet P.[7]	AR	57	M	Indian	Restaurant Owner	1st
Surekha P.[2]	TX	56	F	Indian	Restaurant Owner	-

[1] Interview by Sara Wood, [2] Interview by Amy C. Evans, [3] Interview by Alexis Meza, [4] Interview by Gustavo Arellano,
[5] Interview by Jung Min (Kevin) Kim, [6] Interview by Francis Lam, [7] Interview by Annemarie Anderson

References

Abarca, M.E. (2017) 'Afro-Latina/os' culinary subjectivities: rooting ethnicities through root vegetables', in M. Garcia, E.M. DuPuis, and D. Mitchell (eds) *Food Across Borders*, New Brunswick, NJ: Rutgers University Press, pp 24–43.

Alcorn, C. (2020) 'Coronavirus' toll on Chinese restaurants is devastating', *CNN*, [online] 21 April, Available from: https://www.cnn.com/2020/04/21/business/coronavirus-chinese-restaurants/index.html [Accessed 27 May 2020].

Alkon, A.H., Kato, Y., and Sbicca, J. (2020) *A Recipe for Gentrification: Food, Power, and Resistance in the City*, New York, NY: New York University Press.

Altheide, D.L. (1996) *Qualitative Media Analysis*, Thousand Oaks, CA: SAGE.

Bailey, M. (2018) 'It's not all fried chicken and greasy greens', in S.B. Franklin (ed), *Edna Lewis: At the Table With an American Original*, Chapel Hill, NC: University of North Carolina Press, pp 193–9.

Barnes, S.L. and Blanford-Jones, B. (2019) *The Kings of Mississippi: Race, Religious Education, and the Making of a Middle-Class Black Family in the Segregated South*, New York, NY: Cambridge University Press.

BBV (Barboursville Vineyard). (2007) 'Her Majesty Queen Elizabeth II celebrates the founding of Virginia', *Barboursville Winery*, [Online] 1 June, Available from: https://www.bbvwine.com/news/her-majesty-queen-elizabeth-ii-celebrates-founding-virginia [Accessed 2 May 2020].

Belasco, W. (2002) 'Food matters: perspectives on an emerging field', in W. Belasco and P. Scranton (eds), *Food Nations: Selling Taste in Consumer Societies*, New York, NY: Routledge, pp 2–24.

Beverland, M.B. (2005) 'Crafting brand authenticity: the case of luxury wines', *Journal of Management Studies*, 42(5): 1003–29.

Biery, M.E. (2018) 'Restaurants' margins are fatter, but competition is fierce', *Forbes*, [online] 26 January, Available from: https://www.forbes.com/sites/sageworks/2018/01/26/restaurants-margins-are-fatter-but-competition-is-fierce/#6853b7c727f9 [Accessed 18 March 2020].

Blay-Palmer, A. (2008) *Food Fears: From Industrial to Sustainable Food Systems*, Hampshire, United Kingdom: Ashgate.

Bobo, L.D. and Tuan, M. (2006) *Prejudice in Politics: Group Position, Public Opinion, and The Wisconsin Treaty Rights Dispute*, Cambridge, MA: Harvard University Press.

Bonilla-Silva, E. (2017) *Racism Without Racists: Color-Blind Racism and the Persistence of Racial Inequality in America*, Lanham, MD: Rowman & Littlefield.

Borer, M.I. (2019) *Vegas Brews: Craft Beer and the Birth of a Local Scene*, New York, NY: New York University Press.

Bowen, S., Brenton, J., and Elliott, S. (2019) *Pressure Cooker: Why Home Cooking Won't Solve Our Problems and What We Can Do About It*, New York, NY: Oxford University Press.

Brown, T.B. (2017) 'Muscadines may be the best grapes you've never tasted', *NPR: The Salt*, [online] 26 September, Available from: https://www.npr.org/sections/thesalt/2017/09/26/551835327/muscadines-may-be-the-best-grapes-you-ve-never-tasted [Accessed 11 March 2020].

Burdeau, C. (2015) 'Shrimpers rally in New Orleans against low prices, damage caused by shrimp imports', *The Advocate*, [online] 14 August, Available from: https://www.theadvocate.com/nation_world/article_c8c6a53b-21eb-504f-9828-9f33b4e66fbd.html [Accessed 16 March 2020].

Byrd, K.M. (2019) *Real Southern Barbecue: Constructing Authenticity in Southern Food Culture*, Lanham, MD: Lexington Books.

Cairns, K. and Johnston, J. (2015) *Food and Femininity*, New York, NY: Bloomsbury.

Carolan, M.S. (2011) *Embodied Food Politics*, Burlington, VT: Ashgate.

Carter, A. (2013) 'Virginia wines: in the Old Dominion, a new terroir', *New York Times*, [online] 6 July, Available from: https://www.nytimes.com/2013/07/07/business/virginia-wines-in-the-old-dominion-a-new-terroir.html [Accessed 11 March 2020].

Chefs Collaborative. (ND) 'Seafood solutions', [online] Available from: https://chefscollaborative.org/programs/seafood-solutions/ [Accessed 13 October 2020].

Chen, Y. (2014) *Chop Suey, USA: The Story of Chinese Food in America*, New York, NY: Columbia University Press.

Cockrall-King, J. (2012) *Food and the City: Urban Agriculture and the New Food Revolution*, Buffalo, NY: Prometheus Books.

Cohen, D.T. (2018) 'Coastline county population continues to grow: 60 million live in the path of hurricanes', *The Census*, [online] 6 August, Available from: https://www.census.gov/library/stories/2018/08/coastal-county-population-rises.html [Accessed 16 March 2020].

Collins, K. (2009) *Watching What We Eat: Evolution of TV Cooking Shows*, New York, NY: Bloomsbury.

Conaway, J. (2018) *Napa at Last Light: America's Eden in an Age of Calamity*, New York, NY: Simon and Schuster.

Conway, J. (2020) 'Producing wineries in the U.S. 2020, by state', *Statista*, [online] 10 February, Available from: https://www.statista.com/statistics/259365/number-of-wineries-in-the-us-by-state/ [Accessed 20 May 2020].

Coontz, S. (2006) *Marriage, A History: How Love Conquered Marriage*, New York, NY: Penguin Press.

Cox, K.L. (2008) 'Branding Dixie: the selling of the American South, 1890–1930', in A.J. Stanonis (ed) *Dixie Emporium: Tourism, Foodways, and Consumer Culture in the American South*, Athens, GA: University of Georgia Press, pp 50–68.

DeLind, L.B. (2000) 'Transforming organic agriculture into industrial organic products: reconsidering national organic standards', *Human Organization*, 59(2): 198–208.

Deusing, B. (1996) 'Is organic enough', *Natural Farmer*, 2: 27.

DuCard Vineyards. (ND) 'Virginia wine: what does it mean, deciphering the label', [online] Available from: http://ducardvineyards.com/wp-content/uploads/2018/09/Deciphering_the_label.pdf [Accessed 12 October 2020].

Edge, J.T. (2017) *The Potlikker Papers: A Food History of the Modern South*, New York, NY: Penguin Press.

Edge, J.T. (2020) 'What the coronavirus means for Southern restaurants', *Garden & Gun*, [online] 16 March, Available from: https://gardenandgun.com/articles/what-the-coronavirus-means-for-southern-restaurants/ [Accessed 2 May 2020].

Elliott, D. (2020) '"One alligator apart": pandemic puts new business models on the menu for restaurants', *NPR*, [online] 7 May, Available from: https://www.npr.org/2020/05/07/851539177/one-alligator-apart-pandemic-puts-new-business-models-on-the-menu-for-restaurant [Accessed 27 May 2020].

Engelhardt, E. (2011) *A Mess of Greens: Southern Gender and Southern Food*, Athens, GA: University of Georgia Press.

Estabrook, B. (2011) *Tomatoland: How Modern Industrial Agriculture Destroyed Our Most Alluring Food*, Riverside, NJ: Andrews McMeel.

Fantasia, R. (2010) 'Cooking the books of the French gastronomic field', in E. Silva and A. Warde (eds) *Cultural Analysis and Bourdieu's Legacy*, London, United Kingdom: Routledge, pp 28–44.

Ferris, M.C. (2013) 'The "stuff" of Southern food: food and material culture in the American South', in J.T. Edge, E. Engelhardt, and T. Ownby (eds) *The Larder: Food Studies Methods from the American South*, Athens, GA: University of Georgia Press, pp 276–311.

Ferris, M.C. (2014) *The Edible South: The Power of Food and the Making of an American Region*, Chapel Hill, NC: University of North Carolina Press.

Fine, G.A. (1996) *Kitchens: The Culture of Restaurant Work*, Berkeley, CA: University of California Press.

Finn, S.M. (2017) *Discriminating Taste: How Class Anxiety Created the American Food Revolution*, New Brunswick, NJ: Rutgers University Press.

Franklin, S.B. (2018) 'Introduction', in S.B. Franklin (ed) *Edna Lewis: At the Table With an American Original*, Chapel Hill, NC: University of North Carolina Press, pp 1–14.

Gabaccia, D.R. (2009) *We Are What We Eat: Ethnic Food and the Making of Americans*, Cambridge, MA: Harvard University Press.

Garcia, M., DuPuis, E.M., and Mitchell D. (eds). (2017) *Food Across Borders*, New Brunswick, NJ: Rutgers University Press.

Goffman, E. (1959) *The Presentation of Self in Everyday Life*, Garden City, NJ: Doubleday Anchor.

Green, D. (2019) 'How Whole Foods went from a hippie natural foods store to Amazon's $13.7 billion grocery weapon', *Business Insider*, [online] 2 May, Available from: https://www.businessinsider.com/whole-foods-timeline-from-start-to-amazon-2017-9 [Accessed 22 April 2020].

Griswold, W. (1987) 'A methodological framework for the sociology of culture', *Sociological Methodology*, 17: 1–35.

Harris, D.A. and Giuffre, P. (2015) *Taking the Heat: Women Chefs and Gender Inequality in the Professional Kitchen*, New Brunswick, NJ: Rutgers University Press.

Helmer, J. (2019) 'Why are so many farmers markets failing? Because the market is saturated', *NPR: The Salt*, [online] 17 March, Available from: https://www.npr.org/sections/thesalt/2019/03/17/700715793/why-are-so-many-farmers-markets-failing-because-the-market-is-saturated [Accessed 22 April 2020].

Huber, P. (2008) 'The riddle of the horny hillbilly', in A.J. Stanonis (ed) *Dixie Emporium: Tourism, Foodways, and Consumer Culture in the American South*, Athens, GA: University of Georgia Press, pp 69–86.

Hughes, M. (2000) 'Country music as impression management: a meditation on fabricating authenticity', *Poetics*, 28: 185–205.

The Inn at Little Washington. (2020) 'Philosophy and perspectives', *The Inn at Little Washington Website*, [online] Available from: https://theinnatlittlewashington.com/patrick-oconnell/philosophy-perspectives/ [Accessed 17 April 2020].

Island Free Press. (2020) '2018 a strong, successful year for U.S. fishermen and seafood sector', *Island Free Press*, [online] 24 February, Available from: https://islandfreepress.org/fishing-report/2018-a-strong-successful-year-for-u-s-fishermen-and-seafood-sector/ [Accessed 16 March 2020].

Johnston, J. and Baumann S. (2010) *Foodies: Democracy and Distinction in the Gourmet Foodscape*, New York, NY: Routledge.

Jones, J.A. (2019) *The Browning of the New South*, Chicago, IL: University of Chicago Press.

Jordan, J.A. (2015) *Edible Memory*, Chicago, IL: University of Chicago Press.

Kamp, D. (2006) *The United States of Arugula*, New York, NY: Broadway Books.

Kauffman, J. (2018) *Hippie Food: How Back-to-the-Landers, Longhairs, and Revolutionaries Changed the Way We Eat*, New York, NY: William Morrow Press.

Kavilanz, P. (2020) 'Why this chef keeps showing up at disaster zones', *CNN*, [online] 18 May, Available from: https://www.cnn.com/2020/05/15/business/jose-andres-risk-takers/index.html [Accessed 29 May 2020].

Kerns, M. (2020) 'US seafood consumption rises to highest level since 2007, but falls short of USDA recommendations', *Seafood Source*, [online] 21 February, Available from: https://www.seafoodsource.com/news/supply-trade/us-seafood-consumption-rises-to-the-highest-level-seen-since-2007-but-falls-short-of-usda-recommendations [Accessed 16 March 2020].

Kilman, T. (2011) *The Wild Vine: A Forgotten Grape and the Untold Story of American Wine*, New York, NY: Broadway Books.

Korfhage, M. (2019) 'Fate of 90-year-old Virginia ham smokehouse hangs in balance—and may go to state Supreme Court', *The Virginia-Pilot*, [online] 20 February, Available from: https://www.pilotonline.com/food-drink/article_4925f55a-2bda-11e9-bf8b-cb8b7d3206bb.html [Accessed 8 April 2020].

Latshaw, B.A. (2013) 'The soul of the South: race, food, and identity in the American South', in J.T. Edge, E. Engelhardt, and T. Ownby (eds) *The Larder: Food Studies Methods from the American South*, Athens, GA: University of Georgia Press, pp 99–127.

Levin, J.L., Gilmore, K., Carruth, A., Nonnenmann, M.W., Evert, W., and King, D. (2010) 'An interview with Vietnamese fishermen of Louisiana in the wake of the oil spill', *Journal of Agromedicine*, 15(4): 337–42.

Lippard, C.D. and Stewart, B.E (2019) *Modern Moonshine: The Revival of White Whiskey in the Twenty-First Century*, Morgantown, WV: West Virginia University Press.

Lippert, J., Rosing, H., and Tendick-Matesanz, F. (2020) 'The health of restaurant work: a historical and social context to the occupational health of food service', *American Journal of Industrial Medicine* 63(7): 563–76.

Loffman, M. (2020) 'Asian Americans describe gut punch of racist attacks during coronavirus pandemic', *PBS*, [online] 7 April, Available from: https://www.pbs.org/newshour/nation/asian-americans-describe-gut-punch-of-racist-attacks-during-coronavirus-pandemic [Accessed 27 May 2020].

Ma, A. (2019) 'Nine years later, the BP oil spill's environmental mess isn't gone', *Mother Jones*, [online] 19 April, Available from: https://www.motherjones.com/environment/2019/04/deepwater-horizon-bp-oil-spill/ [Accessed 18 March 2020].

McKee, L.J. (2020) 'A polar vortex delivers frosty weather in some eastern wine regions', *Wine Business*, [online] 11 May, Available from: https://www.winebusiness.com/news/?go=getArticle&dataId=230656 [Accessed 26 May 2020].

McMillan, T. (2012) *The American Way of Eating: Undercover at Walmart, Applebee's, Farm Fields, and the Dinner Table*, New York, NY: Scribner.

Matasar, A.B. (2006) *Women of Wine: The Rise of Women in the Global Wine Industry*, Berkeley, CA: University of California Press.

Michelin. (2020) *The Michelin Guide: Washington DC*, New York, NY: The Michelin Guides.

Miller, A. (2013) *Soul Food: The Surprising Story of an American Cuisine One Plate at a Time*, Chapel Hill, NC: University of North Carolina Press.

Miller, L.J. (2017). *Building Nature's Market: The Business and Politics of Natural Foods*, Chicago, IL: University of Chicago Press.

Myers, L. (2000) 'Cornell students' award-winning business plan will help Virginia farmers replace tobacco with a healthier product: grapes', *Cornell Chronicle*, [online] 26 June, Available from: https://news.cornell.edu/stories/2000/06/plan-tobacco-farmers-grow-grapes [Accessed 11 March 2020].

NC Wine. (2020) 'Starting a winery in North Carolina', North Carolina Department of Agriculture & Consumer Services, [online] Available from: https://www.ncwine.org/starting-a-commercial-winery [Accessed 12 October 2020].

NCMGA (North Carolina Muscadine Grape Association). (2020) 'What are the nutritional benefits of muscadine-grapes wine', North Carolina Muscadine Grape Association, [online] Available from: https://www.ncmuscadinegrape.org/health-benefits/ [Accessed 11 March 2020]

Nosowitz, D. (2015) 'Prices for domestic wild shrimp way down, thanks to foreign farms', *Modern Farmer*, [online] 27 August, Available from: https://modernfarmer.com/2015/08/prices-for-domestic-shrimp-down/ [Accessed 16 March 2020].

O'Brien, E. (2008). *The Racial Middle: Latinos and Asian Americans Living Beyond the Racial Divide*, New York, NY: New York University Press.

Ocejo, R.E. (2017) *Masters of Craft: Old Jobs in the New Urban Economy*, Princeton, NJ: Princeton University Press.

Omi, M. and Winant, H. (2015) *Racial Formation in the United States* (3rd edn), New York, NY: Routledge.

Paxson, H. (2013) *The Life of Cheese: Crafting Food and Value in America*, Berkeley, CA: University of California Press.

Pennell, J.R. (2017) *Local Vino: The Winery Boom in the Heartland*, Urbana, IL: University of Illinois Press.

Peterson, R.A. (1997) *Creating Country Music: Fabricating Authenticity*, Chicago, IL: University of Chicago Press.

Peterson, R.A. (2005) 'In search of authenticity', *Journal of Management Studies*, 42(5): 1083–99.

Peterson, R.A. and Anand, N. (2004) 'The production of culture perspective', *Annual Review of Sociology*, 30(1): 311–34.

Pilcher, J.M. (2012) *Planet Taco: A Global History of Mexican Food*, New York, NY: Oxford University Press.

Portes, A. and Zhou, M. (1992), 'Gaining the upper hand: economic mobility among immigrant and domestic minorities', *Ethnic and Racial Studies*, 15(4): 491–522.

Portes, A. and Zhou, M. (1993) 'The new second generation: segmented assimilation and its variants', *Annals of the American Academy of Political and Social Science*, 530: 74–96.

Purvis, K. (2018) 'One of the South's simplest foods got one of the biggest food awards', *Charlotte* Observer, [online] 10 May, Available from: https://www.charlotteobserver.com/living/food-drink/article210780499.html [Accessed 26 May 2020].

Ray, K. (2016) *The Ethnic Restaurateur*, New York, NY: Bloomsbury.

Reed, J.S. (1986) *The Enduring South: Subcultural Persistence in Mass Society*, Chapel Hill, NC: University of North Carolina Press.

Robinson, J. and Murphy, L. (2013) *American Wine: The Ultimate Companion to the Wines and Wineries of the United States*, Berkeley, CA: University of California Press.

Romero, R. and Harris, D.A. (2019) 'Who speaks for (and feeds) the community? Competing definitions of "community" in the Austin, TX, urban farm debate', *City and Community*, 18(4): 1161–80.

Royster, D.A. (2003) *Race and the Invisible Hand: How White Networks Exclude Black Men from Blue-Collar Jobs*, Berkeley, CA: University of California Press.

Sarmiento, E. (2020) 'Making sense of "local food", urban revitalization, and gentrification in Oklahoma City', in A.H. Alkon, Y. Kato, and J. Sbicca (eds) *A Recipe for Gentrification: Food, Power, and Resistance in the City*, New York, NY: New York University Press, pp 71–90.

Satterthwaite, D. (2009) 'The implications of population growth and urbanization for climate change', *Environment and Urbanization*, 21(2): 545–67.

Schneider, G.S. (2018) 'A sad day in Hamtown: Smithfield Foods closes the only smokehouse making genuine Smithfield Ham', *Washington Post*, [online] 20 July, Available from: https://www.washingtonpost.com/local/virginia-politics/a-sad-day-in-hamtown-smithfield-foods-closes-the-only-smokehouse-making-genuine-smithfield-ham/2018/07/21/dafd57f2-8b7b-11e8-8aea-86e88ae760d8_story.html [Accessed 8 April 2020].

Schneider, M. (2019) 'Most watched television networks: ranking 2019's winners and losers', *Variety*, [online] 26 December, Available from: https://variety.com/2019/tv/news/network-ratings-top-channels-fox-news-espn-cnn-cbs-nbc-abc-1203440870/ [Accessed 19 March 2020].

Sharpless, R. (2010) *Cooking in Other Women's Kitchens: Domestic Workers in the South, 1965–1960*, Chapel Hill, NC: University of North Carolina Press.

Smith, A.F. (2003) 'The first Thanksgiving', *Gastronomica*, 3(4): 79–85.

Southern Foodways Alliance. (2019) 'Oral histories', [online] Available from: https://www.southernfoodways.org/oral-history/ [Accessed 15 February 2019].

Stanonis, A.J. (ed). (2008) *Dixie Emporium: Tourism, Foodways, and Consumer Culture in the American South*, Athens, GA: University of Georgia Press.

Stolberg, S.G. (2016) 'Fire at Virginia smokehouse leaves pork-to-table movement reeling', *New York Times*, [online] 1 February, Available from: https://www.pilotonline.com/food-drink/article_4925f55a-2bda-11e9-bf8b-cb8b7d3206bb.html [Accessed 8 April 2020].

Treitler, V. (2013) *The Ethnic Project: Transforming Racial Fiction into Ethnic Factions*, Stanford, CA: Stanford University Press.

Twitty, M. (2017) *The Cooking Gene: A Journey Through African American Culinary History in the Old South*, New York, NY: Amistad.

VA ABC (Virginia Alcoholic Beverage Control Authority). (2020) 'Farm wineries', [online] Available from: https://www.abc.virginia.gov/licenses/get-a-license/industry-licenses/wine/farm-wineries [Accessed 12 October 2020].

Vazquez-Medina, J.A. (2017) ' "Cooking Mexican": negotiating nostalgia in family owned and small-scale Mexican restaurants in the United States', in M. Garcia, E.M. DuPuis, and D. Mitchell (eds) *Food Across Borders*, New Brunswick, NJ: Rutgers University Press, pp 64–78.

Veseth, M. (2011) *Wine Wars*, Lanham, MD: Rowman & Littlefield.

Weber, M. (2001) *The Protestant Ethic and the Spirit of Capitalism*, London, United Kingdom: Routledge.

Wilcox, M. (2017). 'How chefs are bringing "under-loved" seafood to restaurant menus', *Eater*, [online] 8 September, Available from: https://www.eater.com/2017/9/8/16273592/trash-fish-restaurant-menus-cape-cod [Accessed 13 October 2020].

Wood, L. (2020) 'Global shrimp market projected to cross $24 billion by 2026', *Research and Markets*, [online] 3 March, Available from: https://www.globenewswire.com/news-release/2020/03/03/1994150/0/en/Global-Shrimp-Market-Projected-to-Cross-24-Billion-by-2026-Consumption-Production-Imports-Exports-Industry-Dynamics-Value-Chain-Analysis.html [Accessed 16 March 2020].

WSB-TV. (2018) 'A historical first for heart of Georgia wine country', *WSB Atlanta*, [online] 31 July, Available from: https://www.wsbtv.com/living/travel/a-historical-first-for-heart-of-georgia-wine-country/802836171/ [Accessed 12 October 2020].

Yancey, G. (2003) *Who Is White? Latinos, Asians, and the New Black/Non-Black Divide*, Boulder, CO: Lynne Reinner.

Zecevic, A. (2018) 'Own rooted vs. grafted vines: which makes better wine', *Wine Spectator*, [online] 13 April, Available from: https://www.winespectator.com/articles/do-grafted-or-own-rooted-vines-make-better-wine [Accessed 11 March 2020].

Ziegelman, J. and Coe, A. (2016) *A Square Meal: A Culinary History of the Great Depression*, New York, NY: HarperCollins.

Zukin, S. (1981) *Loft Living: Culture and Capital in the Urban Core*, Baltimore, MD: Johns Hopkins University Press.

Index